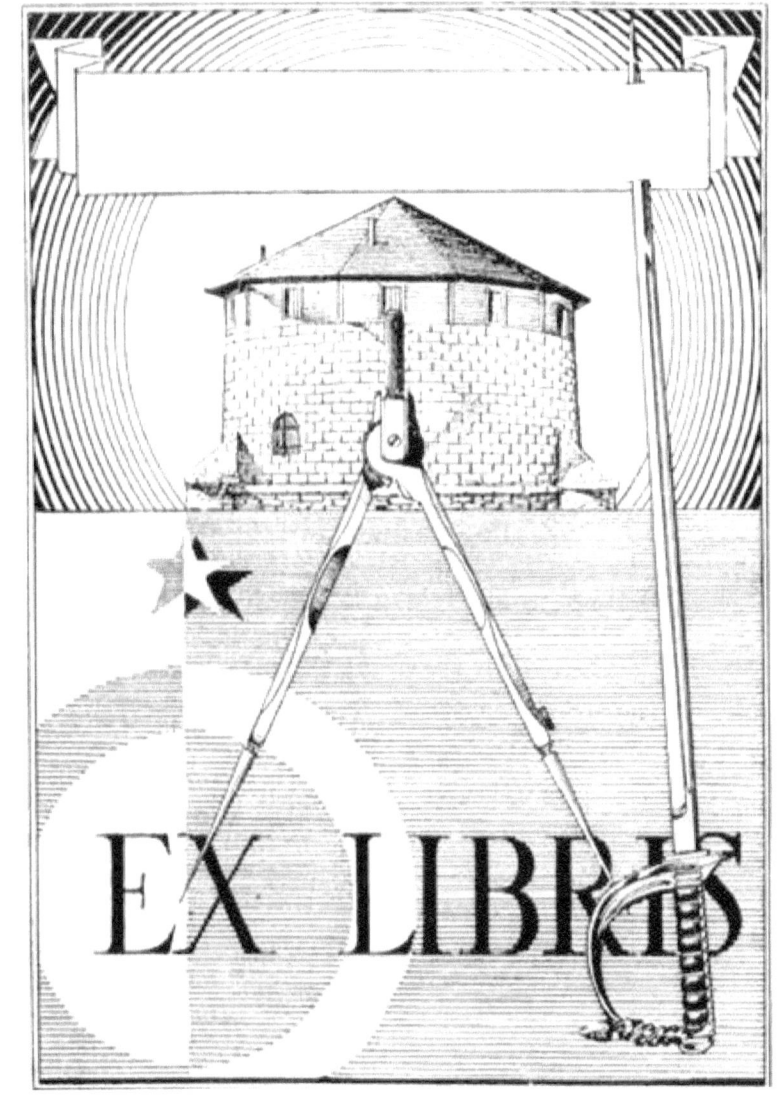

FORGOTTEN ESSAYS
JOSEPH FORT NEWTON 33°
EDITOR:
DARRELL JORDAN, MPS
PUBLISHER: ATHENAIA

Joseph Fort Newton Forgotten Essays - Compiled with graphics and edits by Darrell Jordan, Copyright © First Edition 2024. All rights reserved.
No part of this book may be reproduced in whole or in part without the written permission from the publisher, nor stored in any retrieval system or transmitted by any means, electronic, mechanical, photocopying, recording, or other, without the written consent of the publisher.
For bulk purchases, please contact the publisher.
Enquiry@Athenaia.Co

Library of Congress Cataloging-in Publication Data
Names: Newton, Joseph Fort | Jordan, Darrell
Joseph Fort Newton Forgotten Essays, Darrell Jordan
Description: First U.S. edition. | Coeur D'Alene, Idaho: Athenaia [2024]
Identifiers: LCCN (pending) |
ISBN 979-8-88556-054-2 (First Edition hardcover)
Subjects: REL071000 / RELIGION / Leadership |SOC038000 / SOCIAL SCIENCE / Freemasonry & Secret Societies| PHI036000 / PHILOSOPHY / Hermeneutics
LC record available at https://lccn. loc.gov

On the internet: Parallel47North.com/collections/esoteric-books
Managing Editor: Darrell Jordan
Original Author and Essays: Joseph Fort Newton
Executive Producer: Yuka Jordan
Book Cover Design by Yuka Jordan
Book Cover Art and Illustrations: Jessica Naomi [JessicaNaomiDesigns.com]
Image Credits: Joseph Fort Newton and Darrell Jordan's personal collection
Printed and bound in the United States

Publisher: Athenaia, LLC
2370 N Merritt Crk Lp, Ste 1, Coeur D'Alene, ID 83814
The United States

This book is a collection of select articles from The Builder Magazine during the 4-year period of time Rev. Brother Newton was editor. His intellectual insights still apply today, and we wanted to preserve the precious wisdom of his, and to help you further study Newton's work.

Illustrated Portrait of Joseph Fort Newton

Hand-Drawn by Jessica Naomi

"Employ your time in improving yourself by other men's writings, so that you shall gain easily what others have labored hard for." ~ Socrates

Dedicated to

The Builders of Men, who meet on the Level and part on the Square.

For all his learning or sophistication, man still instinctively reaches toward that force beyond. Only arrogance can deny its existence, and the denial falters in the face of evidence on every hand. In every tuft of grass, in every bird, in every opening bud, there it is. ~ Hal Borland

Table of Contents

Illustrated Portrait of Joseph Fort Newton v

Dedicated to vii

ABOUT JOSEPH FORT NEWTON 10

INTRODUCTION 12

MASONRY AND WORLD-PEACE 15

SOLEMN STRIKES THE FUNERAL CHIME 26

THE SPIRIT OF EASTER 32

EDWIN BOOTH AS A MASON 36

THE FUTURE 42

WAR AND THE MYSTIC TIE 48

THE BIBLE IN MASONRY 51

THE HOUSE OF THE TEMPLE 55

THE PATRIARCHS 57

A FEW OLD BRETHREN 58

YOUNG OLD MEN 59

THE SEVEN AGES OF MAN 61

THE SADDEST THING ON EARTH 62

YOUTH AND AGE 63

HAMLET AND PROSPERO 64

THE HOUSE OF FAITH 66

ARTHUR EDWARD WAITE - AN APPRECIATION 68

EDWIN MARKHAM - POET OF BROTHERHOOD 75

IF A MAN DIE	84
ST. JOHN'S DAY	86
THE MEASURE OF A MAN	89
THE DOCTRINE OF THE BALANCE	92
TRAVEL SKETCHS	99
MARQUIS DE LAFAYETTE	104
TRAVEL SKETCHES	106
THE LAMP OF FELLOWSHIP	113
TRAVEL SKETCHES	116
PRAYER IS TRUST	120
AN AMBASSADOR	132
LINKING ENGLAND AND AMERICA	134
A LEAGUE OF MASONS	137
THE COMMON GOOD	140
THE MYSTIC TIE	144
THE MENS HOUSE	150
EARLY SOCIETY SECRET	152
THE TEMPLE BUILDERS	155
FREEDOM, FRIENDSHIP, FRATERNITY	157
WHAT, THEN, IS MASONRY?	160
Other Books by the Managing Editor	170
About Managing Editor	171

ABOUT JOSEPH FORT NEWTON

Joseph Fort Newton (1876–1950) was an American Baptist minister. He was born in Decatur, Texas, the son of a Baptist minister turned attorney. He attended Southern Baptist Seminary, and Harvard University. While at Harvard he studied under William James. Newton held the honorary degrees of Doctor of Hebrew Literature (Coe College, 1912), Doctor of Divinity (Tufts University, 1919), Doctor of Humane Letters (Hobart and William Smith Colleges, 1926), and Doctor of Laws (Temple University, 1929).

Newton was ordained a Baptist minister in 1895. He held Baptist pastorates in Texas, and led non-sectarian and Universalist congregations in Illinois and Iowa. While in Iowa, he taught English literature at the extension campus of the University of Iowa in Cedar Rapids. While in Cedar Rapids, many of Newton's sermons were published and gained wide circulation. Their popularity in England led him to be called to the pulpit of the City Temple (London) in 1916.

During his four years at City Temple, he made trips throughout the British Isles and gained international fame through sermons in which he urged understanding between England and the United States as a basis of world order and abiding peace. In 1920, Newton returned to the United States and assumed the pulpit at the Church of the Divine Paternity, New York City, NY. While there, Newton served as an editor of the Christian Century, edited the Best Sermons of the Year series, and preached at colleges and universities across the United States.

At the invitation of the Diocese of Pennsylvania Bishop Thomas J. Garland, Newton entered the ministry of the Episcopal Church in September 1925, and came to the

Memorial Church of St. Paul, Overbrook, Philadelphia, PA, as a "special minister." He was ordained as a priest in 1926 at Christ Church, Philadelphia, PA. Newton remained at the Memorial Church of St. Paul until 1930. From 1930 to 1938, Newton assisted the Rev. Dr. John C. H. Mockridge at St. James Church, Philadelphia, PA. In 1938 he assumed the rectorship of Church of St. Luke and The Epiphany, Philadelphia, PA, where he remained until his death in 1950. In 1939, Newton was ranked among the top 5 Protestant Clergyman in the United States. From 1944 until his death, Newton reviewed religious books and wrote a Saturday sermon column for the Philadelphia Evening Bulletin. Newton authored over 30 books, perhaps his most famous being The Builders: A Story and Study of Freemasonry, published in 1914, and translated into six different languages. The Builders is still regarded as one of the best books on the topic.

Masonic History: Rev. Brother Newton became a Master Mason on May 28, 1902, in Friendship Lodge No. 7, Dixon, IL., served the Masonic Grand Lodge of Iowa as its Chaplain from 1911 to 1913, was a 33° Scottish Rite Mason, and an Honorary member of Benjamin Franklin Chapter #105 of National Sojourners. Newton also authored a number of Masonic books, including his best-known works, The Builders (1914), The Men's House (1923), and The Religion of Masonry: An Interpretation (1927). The Builders has been called "an outstanding classic in Masonic literature offering the early history of Freemasonry."

nationalsojourners.org

INTRODUCTION

Our human history, saturated with blood and blistered with tears, is the story of man making friends with man. Society has evolved from a feud into a friendship by the slow growth of love and the welding of man, first to his kin, and then to his kind. The first men who walked in the red dawn of time lived every man for himself, his heart a sanctuary of suspicions, every man feeling that every other man was his foe, and therefore his prey. So, there were war, strife, and bloodshed.

Slowly there came to the savage a gleam of the truth that it is better to help than to hurt, and he organized clans and tribes. But tribes were divided by rivers and mountains, and the men on one side of the river felt that the men on the other side were their enemies. Again, there were war, pillage, and sorrow. Great empires arose and met in the shock of conflict, leaving trails of skeletons across the earth. Then came the great roads, reaching out with their stony clutch and bringing the ends of the earth together. Men met, mingled, passed and repassed, and learned that human nature is much the same everywhere, with hopes and fears in common. Still, there were many things to divide and estrange men from each other, and the earth was full of bitterness. Not satisfied with natural barriers, men erected high walls of sect and caste, to exclude their fellows, and the men of one sect were sure that the men of all other sects were wrong-and doomed to be lost. Thus, when real mountains no longer separated man from man, mountains were made out of molehills-mountains of immemorial misunderstanding not yet moved into the sea!

Barriers of race, of creed, of caste, of habit, of training and interest separate men today, as if some malign genius were bent on keeping man from his fellows, begetting suspicion, uncharitableness, and hate. Still, there are war, waste, and woe! Yet all the while, men have been unfriendly, and, therefore, unjust and cruel, only because they are unacquainted. Amidst feud, faction, and folly, Masonry, the oldest and most widely spread order, toils in behalf of friendship, uniting men upon the only basis upon which they can ever meet with dignity. Each lodge is an oasis of equality and goodwill in a desert of strife, working to weld mankind into a great league of sympathy and service, which, by the terms of our definition, it seeks to exhibit even now on a small scale. At its altar men meet as man to man, without vanity and without pretense, without fear and without reproach, as tourists crossing the Alps tie themselves together, so that if one slips all may hold him up. No tongue can tell the meaning of such a ministry, no pen can trace its influence in melting the hardness of the world into pity and gladness.

The Spirit of Masonry! He who would describe that spirit must be a poet, a musician, and a seer, a master of melodies, echoes, and long, far-sounding cadences. Now, as always, it toils to make man better, to refine his thought and purify his sympathy, to broaden his outlook, to lift his altitude, to establish in amplitude and resoluteness his life in all its relations. All its great history, its vast accumulations of tradition, its simple faith and its solemn rites, its freedom and its friendship are dedicated to a high moral ideal, seeking to tame the tiger in man, and bring his wild passions into obedience to the will of God. It has no other mission than to exalt and ennoble humanity, to bring light out of darkness, beauty out of angularity; to make every hard-won inheritance more secure, every sanctuary more sacred, every hope more radiant!

The Spirit of Masonry! Ay, when that spirit has its way upon earth, as at last it surely will, society will be a vast communion of kindness and justice, business, a system of human service, law, a rule of beneficence; the home will be more holy, the laughter of childhood more joyous, and the temple of prayer mortised and tenoned in simple faith. Evil, injustice, bigotry, greed, and every vile and slimy thing that defiles and defames humanity will skulk into the dark, unable to bear the light of a juster, wiser, more merciful order. Industry will be upright, education prophetic, and religion not a shadow, but a Real Presence, when man has become acquainted with man and has learned to worship God by serving his fellows. When Masonry is victorious, every tyranny will fall, every bastille crumble, and man will be not only unfettered in mind and hand, but free of heart to walk erect in the light and liberty of the truth.

Toward a great friendship, long foreseen by Masonic faith, the world is slowly moving, amid difficulties and delays, reactions and reconstructions. Though long deferred of that day, which will surely arrive, when nations will be reverent in the use of freedom, just in the exercise of power, humane in the practice of wisdom; when no man will ride over the rights of his fellows; when no woman will be made forlorn, no little child wretched by bigotry or greed, Masonry has ever been a prophet. Nor will she ever be content until all the threads of human fellowship are woven into one mystic cord of friendship, encircling the earth and holding the race in unity of spirit and the bonds of peace, as in the will of God it is one in the origin and end. Having outlived empires and philosophies, having seen generations appear and vanish, it will yet live to see the travail of its soul, and be satisfied.

When the war-drum throbs no longer,

And the battle flags are furled;

In the parliament of man,
The federation of the world.

MASONRY AND WORLD-PEACE

HAD anyone written a story of modern civilization last spring, it would have read like a romance. What a picture it would have painted of the triumphs of art and industry, of disease yielding to the skill of science, of the intellectual linking of nations, of the rapid march of ideas, of the annihilation of time and distance by the ingenuities of invention. The bright cities of the earth, with their palaces of art and prayer, lay bathed in sunlight. Air-craft explored the sky, and wireless messages flew every whither, telling of the glory of man.

And then, a high-school boy in remote Bosnia fired a pistol, and a pall of ancient barbaric night fell over the earth, darkening the heavens. Merciful God! The tragedy of it, beyond comparison the greatest war in all the long annals of time in the new century! In an instant, all traces of civilization seemed to vanish, and nation was leaping at the throat of nation, filling the world with measureless misery and woe. Commerce languishes, art is paralyzed, religion is mocked, and civilization seems tumbling into a fall. Four days of the cost of this conflict would dig the Panama Canal and pay for it. One month of it would equip every hospital on earth to fight the great White Plague. Of the loss of life, the most precious of all wealth, who can think without a sob, remembering the cold law of biology by which, if the fittest fall, only the weak remain to father the men of times to be.

What man may ever hope to find words wherewith to tell the shame, the crime, the pity of it all. Prating of Evolution, we were swept along on the crest of an easy optimism, not realizing that we were carrying with us the lower forms of life, "moods of tiger and of ape, red with tooth and claw." Well may we refresh our memories by reading that passage in the "Republic" of Plato, in which a Pagan philosopher laid down the rules of civilized warfare, as follows non-combatants to be spared, no houses to be burned, no farms to be devastated, the dead to be honorably buried, no trophies of war to be placed in the temples of the gods. What a rebuke to Christian civilization in a day when shrines of art and learning and piety are ruthlessly destroyed, and men act like fiends incarnate! Indeed, a page from the story of this war reads like an excerpt from the chronicles of Hell, as witness these words from a war-lord to his men:

"Cause the greatest possible amount of suffering, leave the non-combatants nothing but their eyes to weep with. The law of Christian charity has no bearing on the relation of one nation to another."

With the immediate causes of this world-shaking war, we have not here to do, except to say that no matter what generalization we make about it, there will be found as many facts on one side as on the other. History will debate them for ages to come. Any investigation into the question of who fired the first gun promptly goes back into the question of who made the gun, and why? Who diverted the beautiful, constructive energy of humanity into such wanton waste and unreason? After reading the many-colored books put forth by the nations, each in its own defense, we may admit that all are right in their reasoning's, if we accept their basic fallacy that a nation is a thing apart from humanity to be hedged about with walls of iron.

They are nearer the truth who look for the roots of this tragedy in the ideas taught by unphilosophic philosophers within the last decade or two. Ideas rule the race. They run like rumors, they hide in the crooked lines of a printed page, but in the end, they force us into the arena to fight for them. Materialism in philosophy led, naturally and inevitably, to a worship of brute Force, bringing scientific efficiency to the service of all the horrible gods of sport and speed and splendor. Offering incense to the diabolical trinity of Mammon, Mars, and the Minotaur, we have become so vain of our material advance and scientific technique that we have forgotten that human wellbeing lies in the pursuit of justice and brotherly love. With Nietzsche preaching atheism in the alluring style of a poet, while Treitschke and Bernhardi expounded a rationale, if not a religion, of war, 'tis no wonder that we have been brought to where we are, to a cataclysm unbelievable, except that it exists.

This is not to cry down modern inventiveness and its astonishing achievements. Far from it. Not one of us but feels the thrill of this amazing effort, albeit often futile and misdirected, to realize life. There can be no question that this is a wonderful age, romantic in its advance. Equally, there can be no question that things still more wonderful are to follow. But what is it all worth, this "will to power," this conquest of Nature, if it lead to a wide weltering chaos of world-war? To be sure, we travel more rapidly and get news more quickly, but, God of dreams, what news of savagery and slaughter! No; our ideals are wrong, and with all the suffering and ruin already wrought, maybe it will get into our brains and at last into our hearts, that our real progress does in fact depend on the genuine love of God and our fellow man. Only in tragedy, it seems, will man learn the highest truth.

Still, if we would find the real causes of this dreadful war, we must go far back and deep down into the nature of man. Human history is saturated with blood and blistered with tears. It has been estimated that in the annals of mankind, there have been only thirteen years when there was no war on earth.

"Men are only boys grown tall, Hearts don't change much, after all. Nations are these lads writ large, that's what makes the battle charge."

So reads the record of the ages, and we cannot hope to reverse that order of things in a day. Envy, ignorance, jealousy, greed, hate, revenge, vanity, racial rancor, love of strife, these make war against peace. Nevertheless, we must refuse to accept war as the permanent condition of human society. Slavery was once well-nigh as universal as war, if not as old, but it has been banished from the earth. We cannot look forward very far, but, despite the horror of today, perhaps, indeed, because of it, there is reason to hope for a time when war, and the menace of war, shall be removed from the terrors of human life.

What the issue of this gigantic conflict will be, no mortal can tell. One hundred years ago Europe was swept bare by wars of might against right, yet out of that long-drawn tragedy came a great advance of civilization. So it may be, must be, will be now. Make no mistake; the right will triumph, and as one nation after another is released from the burden of militarism, the arts of peace will prevail, the democratic spirit will be extended, and civilization will, in the end, be promoted. History, always the sure cure for pessimism, holds out this hope even to those, if such there be, who see above its tangled and turbulent scene no vaster, wiser Power correcting the blunders of man, and "from seeming evil still educing good in infinite progression."

Amidst all doubts, one thing is certain: kings may pass, dynasties may vanish, but the peoples of Europe will remain substantially as they are within their historic boundaries. But these battered and impoverished peoples will be preserved for no other purpose than new wars and new disasters if they do not fit themselves with a nobler, truer way of thinking. More important than all else is the question, not as to the map of Europe, but as to what the map of the human mind is going to be after the war. How well men have learned war, reducing it to a fine art of destruction, is shown by those great guns that speak with throats of thunder, and those "airy navies grappling in the central blue," as Tennyson predicted. Now they must learn peace, which means that they must begin with the young, and keep always at it, until mankind masters the sweeter, truer, and diviner language of fraternity.

In point of fact, we have been trying to do an impossible thing, trying to found a humane order upon a basis of brute force. It cannot be done. Long ago, Greece built its structure of art and life upon a basis of slavery, and it fell. Just so, our civilization will fail and fall if it is built upon a foundation of Force. After all, it may be that this war was an inevitable result of a transition from the rule of Force to the rule of Numbers, and, ultimately, the rule of Reason and Love. One is tempted to hope that, since it had to come, it will not stop until all despotisms are swept away, and with them all upholding of the privilege of the few against the rights of the many; until men everywhere rise up and say they will not go to war unless they have a vote on war. John, Hans and mystic Ivan will strike or soon or late, and then will come the end of Kings and Kaisers, and if this war hastens that day, it worth all it cost!

As the grand divisions of geological history have their beginnings in stupendous revolutions, so, too are the great new epochs in the human world. Such a time is even now with us. Manifestly, we stand at the end of an era, and the men who come after us will wonder that, seeing, we saw not, and mistook the red dawn of a new day for a house on fire. As Napoleon would say, we are condemned to something great. Whatever betide, the old order has collapsed. The times are infinitely plastic. There is no reason for letting go of faith in God or humankind. Instead, those who have eyes will see in this tempest a storm that shall clear the air of pestilential vapors and hasten the advent of a nobler world-order, through the corrected sense of the nations, the final flaring up of a blaze from falling brands, to be covered forever with penitential ashes and quenched with bitter tears.

Meantime, what has Masonry to say, what can it do, in this hour of world-crisis when the race is struggling through blood and fire toward something new, shaking off shams, and coming face to face with the eternal necessities? Forming one great society over the whole globe, bringing men together without regard to race or religion, it is incredible that this Ancient Order should be inactive, much less indifferent, in a day of supreme demand. From the first Masonry has been international, knowing no Slavic race, no Teutonic race, but only the Human race, in proof of which hear these words from its Book of Constitutions, words that stand out like stars in the night of world-feud:

"In order to preserve peace and harmony no private piques or quarrels must be brought within the door of the Lodge, far less any quarrel about Religions or National or State-Policy, we being only, as Masons, of the religion in which all men agree; and we are also of all Nations, Tongues, Kindreds and Languages, and are resolved against all Politics as what never yet conduced to the welfare of the Lodge, nor ever will.

Such is the principle on which Masonry rests, and the spirit in which it has toiled through the ages, breaking down barriers of caste and creed, of race and rank, creating reverence, not only for the Divine, but also for the Human, for man as man, regardless of land or language, for the right of every man to be free of body and soul and have a place in the sun, and drawing men together in mutual respect into a profound and far-reaching fellowship. Never was its benign spirit more needed than today, living, as we are, in a world of fratricidal strife, when every energy of the race seems dedicated to destruction. Alas, that the truth of the Brotherhood of Man should be revealed only in tragedy and terror, but if the sword of Mars stabs the worldwide awake to this fact, by the very magnitude of the horror of war, it will be worth the price in suffering. Truly, the time has come when Masonry must take up its harp and strike its world-chord with all its might, strike it magnificently and with prophetic stroke.

Human unity is no fanciful dream of a poet, no far off promise of a prophet; it is a fact. Geographical boundaries do not now and never have represented either race or national potencies. Morality, intelligence, efficiency, fraternity refuse racial or political labels. There is no German chemistry, no British astronomy, no Russian mathematics. What is most excellent in Russia, its Tolstoys, its Kropotkins, its musicians, its painters, and its hard-handed millions of toilers, is not Russian, but human. The same is true of Germany, France and England. Goethe and Schiller, Koch and Kant are fellow-countrymen of Shakespeare and Darwin, of Hugo and Pasteur. The Republic of Letters and of Science is universal; it is only our patriotism that has lagged behind and become "the virtue of narrow minds" when, indeed, it is not actually what Johnson called it, "the last resort of knaves."

How, then, can we justify our love of our own land as over against those who hold that all patriotism is provincial, if not pernicious? Only in this way: Each nation, each race has a genius of its own, and by that fact a contribution to make and a service to render to the total of humanity. Judea was no larger than Iowa, and yet it gave to the race its loftiest and truest religion, and the strongest, whitest, sweetest soul the earth has known. Greece was a tiny land, girt about by violet seas, but it added immeasurable wealth of art, drama and philosophy to the world. So, of Rome. And thus, we might call the roll of races and nations, asking of each what it had or has to give of beauty and of truth to mankind. Even so, our country has a genius unique, particular, and peculiar, and by that token a service to render to the universal life of humanity. What is that service if it be not to show, not only that "government of the People, by the People, for the People shall not perish from the earth," but that it is the highest ideal of government, and that it makes for the greatest happiness of man, alike in private nobility and public welfare? Of that genius and service, our flag is the emblem and prophecy, and loyalty to that emblem implies devotion to that service. Our field is the world, but our solicitude is our own country that it may the better make its unique and priceless contribution to the universal good. Thus, with due reverence for other nations, by loyalty to our own flag, we best serve our race.

Above all nations, greater than all races, more important than all royalties is Humanity, and no one nation can live to itself, much less be truly great, without regard for the usefulness and happiness of other nations. What we need is a transvaluation of patriotism from a tribal loyalty into a universal allegiance, a world patriotism, growing out of the deepening sense of human solidarity, large of outlook, far-reaching and benign of spirit. As it is now, patriotism consists too much in loving our own land and hating every other a feeling unworthy of a Republic where Teuton, Saxon, Slav, Gaul, Celt live amicably together, stand shoulder to shoulder in the industrial army, eat out of the same dinner pails, and, to a surprising degree, worship at the same altar.

Exactly, and that is the very genius of Freemasonry, its mission to mankind, and the spirit which it seeks to make prevail. By its very nature cosmopolitan, it thinks in terms of Humanity, rather than of race or creed or party, being as the old German Handbook defined it, the activity of closely united men who, employing symbolical forms borrowed from architecture work for the welfare of humanity, striving morally to ennoble themselves and others, and thereby to bring about "a universal league of mankind, which they aspire to exhibit, even now, on a small scale." As Goethe said, in his poem on "The Lodge,"

"The Mason's ways are

A type of existence,

And his persistence

Is, as the days are

Of men in this world."

Every Lodge is an emblem and prophecy of the world, and there will be no abiding peace on earth until what Masonry exhibits on a small scale is made worldwide, and its spirit of goodwill among men of all ranks, races and religions becomes the reigning genius of humanity. Other way out of war there is none. If, instead of meeting behind closed doors for intrigue, the men who plotted this war had met in a Masonic Lodge, not one of them would have drawn a sword! Alas, Lilliputian militarists have kindled a fire which not even Gulliver can put out, spreading death and desolation every whither-fanning old feuds, marshalling hordes of hates, until the very existence of civilization is threatened.

What of the future? One thing is evident: if this tragedy drags its bloody way to the bitter end, as now seems likely, every tie by which man is bound to man the world over will be needed to hold the race together; and Masonry is one of those ties. To that end, Masonry itself must recapture its old accent and emphasis upon universal principles, and take part in recruiting and mobilizing a great army of men of goodwill, if so, we may dehorn the nations now goring each other to death, and bring to this passion-clouded earth the light of reason. War is waste. It is unreason. It settles nothing. It is devolution, not evolution. It is not the survival of the fittest, but the sacrifice of the best. The canker of long peace, as Shakespeare called it, is the canker not of peace, but of materialism. No;

"The crest and crowning of all good,

Life's final star, is Brotherhood;

For it will bring again to Earth

Her long-lost Poesy and Mirth;

Will send new light on every face,

A kingly power upon the race.

And till it comes we men are slaves,

And travel downward to the dust of graves."

What this sad world needs is a League of its "Large Eternal Fellows," tall enough of soul to look over barriers of race, walls of creed, and mountains of misunderstanding, and recognize their kinsmen in every land and language. These are the men who see that we are in more danger from the grasping greed and blind ambition of the few who rule than we ever were, ever will or ever can be from the great, toiling masses of our fellows in other lands. They see that the great generalship displayed in the war, and its good comradeship, the sagacity of its leaders, and the singing, jesting courage with which the youth of Europe is marching to the grave are the very qualities which, if dedicated to the organization of the world upon a basis of peace, will swing the earth into a new orbit! Therefore;

> *"Come, clear the way, then, clear the way:*
>
> *Blind creeds and kings have had their day.*
>
> *Break the dead branches from the path:*
>
> *Our hope is in the aftermath*
>
> *Our hope is in heroic men,*
>
> *Star-led to build the world again,*
>
> *To this event the ages ran:*
>
> *Make way for Brotherhood make way for Man!*

SOLEMN STRIKES THE FUNERAL CHIME

HOW many tender memories these old familiar words evoke in the mind of a Mason. Often in the open lodge alas, all too often beside the open grave, he has heard them march with slow, majestic step to the measure of the Pleyel Hymn. Never were words and melody more fitly blended, and they induce a mood pensive indeed, but not plaintive, rich in pathos without being poignant, a mood of sweet sadness caught at that point where it stops short of bitter, piercing grief. Yet few know when it was written and by whom, though many must have paused to muse over the faith of which it sings.

The hymn was written by David Vinton, a lecturer on Masonry and teacher of the ritual in the first quarter of the last century, whose field of labor was in the South, chiefly in North Carolina. Unfortunately, his path through life was dogged by the demon of drink, which left stains upon his character for which he was expelled by a Lodge in North Carolina. He died, so Mackey records, in Shakertown, Kentucky, in July, 1833, but Morris dates his death six years earlier and says that it occurred near Russellville, Ky. Morris adds this pathetic fact: "Nor were his own most beautiful words sung over his grave, on account of lapse from a life of sobriety."

In 1816 Vinton issued a volume entitled "The Masonic Minstrel, a Selection of Masonic, Sentimental, and Amorous Songs. Duets, Glees, Canons, Rounds and Canzonets, Respectfully Dedicated to the Most Ancient and Honorable Fraternity of Free and Accepted Masons," with an appendix containing a short historical sketch of Masonry and a list of all the Lodges in the United States. It was printed for the author by H. Mann and Company,

Dedham, Mass., and more than twelve thousand copies were sold to the Craft. This volume contained his funeral dirge set to the melody of the Pleyel hymn. As Mackey remarks, "This contribution should preserve the name of Vinton among the Craft, and in some measure atone for his faults, whatever they may have been."

From the preface of the Minstrel, we learn that Vinton was appointed by Mount Vernon Lodge, in Providence, to procure a book of songs for use in the Lodge, and this suggested the book to his mind, the more so when he was unable to find any book to meet the need. This quaint volume, yellow with age, and alternating quickly from grave to gay, from lively to severe, tempts comment, did time permit; but our concern here is only with his dirge. Originally it had eight stanzas, only four of which are used in our ritual and burial service, and Vinton little thought that his lines would be sung for a decade, then laid aside, then taken up again and sung wherever a Brother Mason is laid to rest, "in the land called America."

Whether we hear this hymn in the tyled recesses of the Lodge, or on a green sward out under the sky, our hearts answer to its appeal. Albeit in less stately strain and more tender tone, it strikes the same note that sounds through the 90th Psalm that mighty funeral hymn of the human race with its chant of the swift death of mourning flowers, of the vanishing of man, and the hush of profound sleep to which all things mortal decline. How helpless man is, pursued by Time and overtaken by Death his life a vapor that melts, his span of years a tale that is soon told. There is here that nameless sorrow, that unutterable sadness which lingers in all mortal music whatsoever, and will linger in it while yet we walk in the dim country of this world where Death seems to divide divinity with God. Evermore, in hours, however trivial or tragic, in moods pensive or gay.

> *"Solemn strikes the funeral chime,*
> *Notes of our departing time;*
> *As we journey here below,*
> *Through a pilgrimage of woe."*

Touched by the twilights of time, the singer meditates and prays. He sees that the vast machinery of Nature carries forward the entire human race, and, without fail, drops them into one final sleep. Yet each departs alone: the father without the child, the wife without the husband, the judge without the court, the statesman unattended, the babe with no arm around it, aye, and king and peasant alike; and all walk one dark, inevitable path. In what silence and dignity, they go, their faces all turned in one direction, following the footprints of a many millioned multitude into the infinite. We who are compelled to watch their moving figures are powerless to detain them, and can only say farewell and then weep.

> *"Mortals now indulge a tear,*
> *For mortality is here;*
> *See how wide her trophies wave,*
> *O'er the slumbers of the grave."*

With all our philosophy and wit, death remains a bitter, old, and haggard fact which no man may either evade or avert. There is something appalling in the masterful negation and collapse of the body. It is profound. It is pathetic. Words are futile, and there is in that last silence what makes them seem foolish. What avails it what any man may have to say about death? The real question is, what are we to say to it, whether or not we shall let it have the last word.

> *"Not all the preaching since Adam*
> *Has made Death other than Death."*

Heart and flesh fail; and the generations come and go, following the forlorn march of dust. Truly, as for man, his days are as grass; as a flower of the field, so he flourisheth; for the wind passeth over it, and it is gone.

Suddenly the shadow lifts, light shineth in darkness, and we see how true it is that the soul of man is the one unconquerable thing upon this earth. How wonderful is this ancient, high, heroic faith which refuses to admit that the grave is the gigantic coffin lid of a dull and mindless universe descending upon it at last. Life tries it, sorrow beshadows it, sin stains it, and yet it is victorious. When doubt deepens this faith becomes more profound, and out of the blackest tragedy, it rises with a song of triumph. So, it has been from the far time when the oldest book in the world was written, and so it will be until whatever is to be the end of things.

> *"Here, another guest we bring;*
> *Seraphs of celestial wing,*
> *To our funeral altar come;*
> *Waft a friend and brother home."*

Such faith is not a mere surrender; it is a force prophetic of its own fulfillment. At its touch the graveyard becomes a cemetery that is, a sleeping chamber, and dark

Death an All-Man's Inn where a fellow pilgrim takes lodging for a night. Those whom we call the dead are the guests of God, whose love is the keeper of unknown revelations. Also, our singer sees that the social life of man, its warmth of sympathy, its sanctity of friendship, its dear love of man for his comrade, has enduring value. Because this is so; because life is brief at its longest, and broken at its best, it must be filled with Truth and Love; that so we may bring to the Gate in the Mist something too noble to die. Hence the wise prayer:

"Lord of all below, above,

Fill our souls with Truth and Love;

As dissolves our Earthly Tie,

Take us to Thy Lodge on High."

O Death, where is thy victory? Our trust is in God, that He who made us what we are will lead us to what we ought to be. Higher faith, there is none. Even so, Masonry rests its hope upon the ultimate Reality, the first truth and the last, and it is therefore that its singer sees, amidst the fluctuating shadows of this twilight world, an august, incomprehensible destiny for man. As a song of triumph, the four stanzas omitted from this historic hymn are worthy of remembrance:

"For beyond the grave there lie

Brighter mansions in the sky!

Where, enthroned, the Deity

Gives man immortality.

There, enlarged, his soul will see
What was veiled in mystery;
Heavenly glories fill the place,
Show his Maker face to face.

God of life's eternal day!
Guide us, lest from Thee we stray,
By a false, delusive light,
To the shades of endless night.

Calm, the good man meets his fate,
Guards celestial round him wait;
See! he bursts these mortal chains,
And o'er death the victory gains."

THE SPIRIT OF EASTER

ONCE again, borne on that tide of Eternity which men call Time, we have come to the great day of Memory and Hope. That a day in Spring should be set apart to commemorate the ever-renewed evidence of the Life Everlasting is in accord with the fitness of things, as if the seasons of the soul were attuned to the seasons of the year. It is more than beautiful; it unites faith with life, linking the fresh buds of returning spring with the ancient poetries and pieties of the human heart. It finds in Nature, with her woven hymns of night and day, of winter and summer, a ritual of prophecy and joy.

A breath we are, servile to all skyey influences, said the prince of poets; and something in the stir of life in the reviving earth, in the springtime overflowing the world like a heavenly Nile, in the resurrection of the tender race of flowers, begets an unconscious, involuntary renewal of the faith of man, refreshing his hope and quickening his passion for life. So, we look into the face of the new spring and our hearts are strangely glad, and strangely sad, also touched by dim, wistful memories of springs agone when life was new and we were young; melted by "the song of those who answer not, however we may call." So run the records of all the times, since ever Time began, and so it will be until the last man lifts his trembling hands in prayer on this dying earth. Nor is it a mere fancy that has thus prompted our humanity to greet the coming of spring with feast and festival, as symbolizing the victory of life over the white winter of death, for in Nature there is no death, but only living and living again.

Admit that Easter is an old sun-feast, a spring frolic, or whatever else wise men may dig up from the folklore of olden time, it is for us the Feast of Christ none the less, and there is in it that touch of melancholy in joy which all lovers of the Christ feel is the note of His life as it sounds in the story of pilgrimage, in the tone of His words, and in the pathos of His passion. Think as we may of that tragic and heroic Figure, this is the day of Jesus, whose Life of Love is the one everlasting romance in this prosaic old world, and whose ineffable tenderness seems to blend naturally with the thrill of springtime when the finger of God is pointing the new birth of the earth. Our little passions are as naught in the face of that mighty Passion; our small trials fade before that solemn trial of Love and Death; and we are subdued with a sense of something as far beyond our useful tasks or transient joys, as the awakening of Nature is beyond our waking from slumber.

No other day touches us more deeply, more tenderly, more joyously, and none so stirs the spirit of hope and courage in the heart of man. Hope and courage we have for the affairs of daily life, albeit a courage that is often faint, and a hope that is not hopeless, but unhopeful; but here is a Hope that leaps beyond the borders of the world, and a Courage that faces Eternity! For that Easter stands; in its history, its music, its springing earth, its prophecy of renewal for the putting off of the tyranny of Time, the terror of the Grave, and the triumph of the Flesh, and the putting on of Immortality. It is thus that Easter gives us the hint, if not the key, to a higher heroism and cheer, that which Tennyson meant when he wrote that rather than the glory of warrior, the glory of orator, the glory of song, "give me the glory of going on and still to be" a glory which puts a new meaning and value on life with its efforts, so sadly baffled; its acquirements, so incomplete; its achievements, so transient and so quickly forgotten. For we can work with brave hearts, and endure with serenity, and delight without alloy, if the good we aim at here, and never quite attain, is an earnest of the Good we shall win other where.

It profits us little to argue amid music and flowers, or at any other time in respect of this high confidence. The faith of Easter has its home in the deep heart of man for the Heart hath its reasons which the Reason knows not of and it is older than all arguments, which are only so many efforts of logic to justify to the reason the faith of the soul. No man was ever argued into this Faith, or out of it. Its roots go deeper than argument, deeper than dogma, deeper than reason, ay, as deep as the home and the family, as deep as infancy and old age, as deep as love and death! As we do not ask logic to prove the coming of Spring, so there is no need that anyone argue in behalf of the faith older than history that the mysterious Power which weaves in silence robes of white for the lily, of red for the rose, will the much more clothe our winged spirits with a moral beauty that shall never fade.

> *"What to you is Shadow, to Him is Day,*
>
> *And the end He knoweth;*
>
> *And not on a blind and aimless way*
>
> *Thy spirit goeth.*
>
> *The steps of Faith*
>
> *Fall on a seeming void, and find*
>
> *A Rock beneath."*

Let those doubt who will, it is still true that the Spirit of Christ does live in the hearts of a multitude, some of them all unaware, in deeds of love and pity all the world over. And His great and simple words, as those of no other, do uplift and fortify the soul against the fear of that Shadow that waits for every man. The only things worth our while are the things thought and felt and done in accord with His spirit and example, in sympathy with His life so serene, so radiant, so triumphant. The sorrow is that we for whom He lived and died, by our misdeeds, by our falling away from His ideal, crucify the Man we ought to be many times again. Yet is there hope, though we have fallen far and fallen low hope in God whom He revealed as our Father, whose love hath in it the secret of unknown redemptions. Sorrows come, and deep grief, and loneliness unutterable, when those whom we love fall into the great white sleep; but the Easter Lily will grow in our hearts if we cultivate it, watering it the while with our tears, and at last it will bloom, and its beauty will be the fairest thing in the house of our pilgrimage.

> *"If Jesus Christ is a man,*
>
> *And only a man I say*
>
> *That of all mankind I cleave to Him,*
>
> *And to Him I cleave always.*
>
> *If Jesus Christ is a God*
>
> *And the only God I swear*
>
> *I will follow Him through heaven and hell,*
>
> *The earth, the sea, and the air."*

EDWIN BOOTH AS A MASON

IN an earlier issue reference was made to a statue of Edwin Booth, the great master of tragedy, recently erected in Gramercy Park, near the Players Club, of which Booth was the founder. Designed by E. T. Quinn who also wrought the bust of Poe, in Poe Park it reveals the vanished actor in his favorite role of Hamlet, which temperament, training and personality had made peculiarly his own. Believing that his readers would like to know more about Booth, both as a man and a Mason, ye editor has made some research among his relatives and friends, the results of which he offers herewith, along with certain observations on a man who was as noble in his life as he was great in his art.

Those who wish to know the story of Booth in detail, and a memorable story it is, worthy of being told many times may find it recorded with exquisite insight and skill in the "Life and Art of Edwin Booth," by William Winter, the Plutarch of our stage. Truly, it is a fascinating book, as much for its descriptions of Booth on the stage as for its account of his habits in private life for, in the art of interpreting the personality of an artist, there is no one like Winter, no one near him. Such genius is rare, and the more precious for that the art of a great actor dies with him, save as it may live, for a brief time, in the minds of the generation before whom he appears. Happily, an intimate fellowship united with literary power to preserve the image and art of Booth, and to these was added life-long love of the man as witness these words:

"*Farewell; nor mist, nor flying cloud,*
Nor night can ever dim

The wreath of honors pure and proud,
Our hearts have twined for him!"

Spiritual personality eludes definition; to be is more than to do, and the soul of Edwin Booth was greater even than his achievement. He was a benefactor to thousands, revealing to them, now in forms of beauty and color, now in shapes of terror and power, the wonder of human nature and its destiny. By birth and heredity, he possessed those qualities of beauty, grace, charm and expression which others strive in vain to attain. His face, his voice, his gesture, and his brilliant and beautiful spirit gave him conquest those dark eyes flashing divine fire, not alone of physical vitality, but of imagination, emotion, and exaltation of soul. He had no need of novelties; he was himself a novelty. In Richelieu, Othello, Iago, Lear, Bertuccio, and Brutus, but most of all, in Hamlet, his power was made manifest; power of insight, of intense emotion, of richness and color of personality, of thoughtful, brooding habit of a stately mind all abstracted from passion and suffused with a mysterious melancholy and the pensive, dreamlike soul of a poet. Such qualities made his Hamlet an unforgettable picture of sorrowful grandeur, sad majesty, ineffable mournfulness, and grief-stricken isolation, as of one who walked a troubled way amid the foul crimes of the living and the phantoms of the dead. Whether in the glittering halls of Elsinore, on its midnight battlements, or in its lonely wind beaten place of graves, the lovely, suffering, awestruck spirit of the Prince seemed to wear once more his robe of flesh.

In private life Booth was the soul of honor, gentle, affable, often playful, and uncommonly apt in telling comic stories, albeit men felt that he dwelt somewhat apart and aloof sometimes mistaking an excess of modesty for haughtiness, whereas beneath his reserve there was an abundance of kindness and good fellowship. As a son, he was tenderly devoted, thoughtful of everything that could solace the declining years of an aged mother, provident of blessings, tireless in service; and his reverence for the memory of his father was akin to religion. A devout Christian in faith, he had, nevertheless, a foreboding nature, and expected every kind of disaster except the most terrible one of all which befell him when his brother murdered Lincoln. It was pitiful to see him then, bowed low under the shadow of a tragedy greater than he had portrayed on the stage. Youth goes; age comes; and Booth passed into the sear and yellow leaf with dignity and sweetness, and never knew "the set gray life and its apathetic end."

Of his Masonic fellowship, his brother-in-law, J. H. Magonigle, writes: "Yes, Edwin Booth was an ardent Mason, and for twenty-five years before his death, on June 7th, 1893, was a member of New York Lodge, No. 330. He was always proud of the Fraternity, but the exactions of his profession prevented his regular attendance at Lodge. For the same reason, he was kept from being the Master of a Lodge of Masons, which was one of his dearest ambitions. Nevertheless, the Brethren held him in high esteem and were proud of his association." Brother A. A. Auchmoedy gives this interesting reminiscence:

"I was Master of a Masonic Lodge in Omaha a good many years ago. Edwin Booth was playing in the city. I knew that he was a Mason, and sent a committee over to invite him to meet with us after the play. He sent back word that he would do so with pleasure, and we sent a committee to escort him to the Lodge. The examination was brief, but entirely satisfactory, and when he entered the room, every member was on his feet, greeting him with hearty applause. He seemed much interested in the closing exercises, and at the banquet which followed, he was a happy member of the party. There were songs, in which

Booth joined heartily with his wondrously sweet voice, and several brief speeches before the great actor was called upon. He began by saying:

'Mr. Toastmaster and Brothers: I am like a boy out-of-school tonight. It is a delight to be with you. If I act like a boy, kindly overlook it.' Then he told many interesting stories of his connection with Masonry and of his career as an actor how deeply grateful he had been at the forethought and tender consideration of his brethren in times of great distress, hinting at the days when he felt himself under a cloud, when President Lincoln met his death at the hands of his brother. Continuing, he said: 'I shall never forget that wherever I went Masons rallied about me and cheered my drooping spirits. But for their love and forethought I can tell you now, my Brethren, I do not think I should have resumed my life as an actor after that awful event.'

Suddenly he switched to a pleasantry, and had all of us laughing. His readings seemed brighter and better than they ever were on the stage. One Brother asked him what was his favorite poem, and after thinking a moment, he answered: 'Please put the question differently, and ask me what my favorite hymn is.' We all wondered what it would be. Then, in a voice low and sweet, he said: 'That hymn which the world knows as Jesus Lover of My Soul' and without waiting, he recited it as we had never heard it recited before. A member asked for his favorite piece of prose:

'I thank you, my Brother,' he said, 'for asking that question. The most beautiful, impressive, noble, and unforgettable and uplifting words that were ever uttered and preserved to the world, I shall do myself the honor of reciting. Please be standing with me.' And with bowed head he recited the Lord's Prayer."

Naturally, it was the dramatic element in Masonry that attracted the attention of a man like Booth, and he never ceased to wonder at the simplicity, power, and firm grip on the bitter, old and dark reality of life displayed in the drama of the Third Degree. Surely he was no mean judge of tragedy, and he left this testimony:

"In all my research and study, in all my close analysis of the masterpieces of Shakespeare, in my earnest determination to make those plays appear real on the mimic stage, I have never, and nowhere, met tragedy so real, so sublime, so magnificent as the legend of Hiram. It is substance without shadow the manifest destiny of life which requires no picture and scarcely a word to make a lasting impression upon all who can understand. To be a Worshipful Master, and to throw my whole soul into that work, with the candidate for my audience and the Lodge for my stage, would be a greater personal distinction than to receive the plaudits of the people in the theatres of the world."

Toward the end, Booth lived much alone reading, musing, pondering upon his art, and, especially, thinking of that one other subject which engaged him most deeply Religion. He had the constant spirit of a believer, the impartiality of a philosopher, and the soul of a poet; and so, whether in youth or age, diffused an influence of strength, grace, and peace. The charm of his nature was blended composure, gentleness, and power. Upon the marge of that vast mystery which encircles our little lives like a sea, he stood in awe, wonder, and confidence and so drifted away. Around his name is a halo of romance that will never fade. His character and conduct are summed up in the words of Hamlet to Horatio, which he once wished might be his epitaph:

"Thou hast been
As one, in suffering all, that suffers nothing,
A man that Fortune's buffets and rewards
Hast taken with equal thanks."

THE FUTURE

WHAT is to be the future of Freemasonry? With increasing frequency, this question is being asked in Masonic gatherings, and in one form or another it comes to ye editor almost every day in the letters that pour into his office. Save in a few instances, due to impatience, the spirit in which it is asked is not radical, much less revolutionary. Nevertheless, it is earnest, insistent, and profoundly significant. It does not mean that men are losing or have lost faith in Masonry, but that they are beginning to realize its latent power and its hitherto unguessed possibilities as an instrument for social service and the betterment of humanity.

There are those who regret, if they do not actually resent, the spirit of restlessness which more and more prevails in the Fraternity in respect to its future. Surely that is shortsightedness. What we should rather deplore is an attitude of settled self-satisfaction and smug complacency with things as they are. Everything advances, improves, broadens, and Masonry must keep step with the march of mankind, or step aside. An institution that does not, will not, or cannot adapt itself to the conditions and demands of the new and changed time in which we live, is doomed. Today thousands of men, especially young men, are asking of Masonry the very same question which she asked of them when they knocked at her door: Whence came you and what came you here to do? They are not irreverent. They are not radical iconoclasts. But they know that the demand of this age is for efficiency, and they are eager to have a part in making Masonry effective in the fulfillment of the great purpose for which it exists.

Between those who will let nothing alone and those who will allow nothing to be improved, there is a middle path of cautious progress and development. John Bright held it to be the study of a wise statesman to "make the past glide easily and safely into the future, without loss"; with which agrees the wisdom of Burke that the useful man is he who has "the disposition to conserve and the ability to improve." For, if we do not conserve what we have we cannot improve it, or apply it. Nor can we really conserve it without constantly improving and applying it. But we must have not only the wish but also the knowledge and ability to improve, else we shall lose what we have in blunderingly trying to get what we want. Therefore, if our young men are to serve Masonry and make it effective for its high end, they must be taught what Masonry is, whence it came, what it brought to us from the past, and what it is trying to do in this tangled and turbulent world. So, and only so, can they wisely conserve its holy and historic tradition and apply its spirit and teachings to the problems of the present.

Everywhere the signs of an awakening of the Masonic Spirit multiply, and for no gift of the Almighty, whose inspiration has given man understanding, ought we to be more grateful. Just because this is so; because the Craft hears the call of great opportunity, and feels the pressure of far-reaching demands, we must keep our minds clear and our hearts responsive, lest we be swept too far in one direction or turn aside into another. As for ye humble editor, he must confess that in regard to the fundamental principle and purpose of Masonry, he is a standpatter who cannot be moved. For that very reason, in regard to the improvement and application of Masonry, the effort to make its ritual more radiant, its symbolism more luminous, its philosophy more understandable, its spirit more active and its labors more practical and efficient, he is a progressive who cannot be stopped. What is more, he is sure that this is the attitude of the great majority of the Craft, and that we are on the eve of a new day in Masonry.

This at least is manifestly true, as one of the ablest of our Masonic students puts it in a thoughtful letter: "Masonry ought to be more than a social club, or a dramatic society, or a charity institute, or a building association. Maybe it ought to be all these things, but it must be something more." Exactly; and he might have added that it is that Something More which has made Masonry what it is, preserved it through the ages, winning to it the homage and loyalty of brave and true men; and that Something More by which we mean its sweet spirit of Brotherly Love, the wise Faith which it inspires, the simple Truths which it teaches, the passion for Liberty and Equality which it evokes, and the noble Spirituality which it cultivates will yet make it what it ought to be, conserving its heroic tradition and giving shape to its future. More than an institution, more than a tradition, more than a society Masonry is one of the forms of the Divine Life upon earth; and a spirit so benign and beautiful, an influence so quiet and unresting, was never more needed than today.

Three paths would seem to be open to our Order, two of which are full of promise of fruitful achievement, and one, alas, dark with danger. First of all, Masonry can go on as it is, working quietly in behalf of unity, amity and friendship among men, bringing men of differing faiths and types of mind and effort together at its altar of light and prayer, the while it teaches them in parable, symbol and drama the truths that make it worth our time to live and let live, think and let think. Forming one great society over the whole round earth a fraternity of free men, founded upon moral truth and spiritual faith its mission is to make men friends, to refine and exalt their lives, to turn them from bigotry and falsehood to charity and love of truth. While not a religion, it religiously holds the right and duty of every man to worship in the way his heart loves best, granting to every other man the like precious privilege. Holding aloof from separate sects and parties, it lays emphasis upon the things that underlie all creeds and overarch all sects, seeking to bring about that great fellowship of humanity in which God is most truly found and known. Truly, no more worthy purpose can inspire any order than the earnest, active endeavor to bring men into closer fellowship with one another and with spiritual reality. This is as much needed today as ever before, and if Masonry did nothing else, it would be entitled to the gratitude of humanity.

> *"What might be done? This might be done,*
> *And more than this, my suffering Brother,*
> *More than the tongue*
> *E'er said or sung,*
> *If men were wise and loved each other!"*

Unfortunately, another path lies very near our feet just now, and many Masons are sorely tempted to take it, owing to the aggressive activity of influences which threaten, as they think, all that they hold dear. No doubt the provocation is great, and even a blind man a tree can see the facts which fill them with alarm, albeit he may also see how easily those facts may be undignified or distorted by anger and alarm. Admit that the facts are as dark as they are depicted, still there remains the question as to how we can best meet them, what should be our spirit and method. Fighting evil with evil is the ultimate folly. Not only does it fail, but the fighters become infected by the virus of the enemy whom they would overthrow, and so in the end are themselves overthrown. Every man and Mason will act when he is needed in the cause of liberty and righteousness, afraid of no one, quarrelling with no one, alert, wary, and without compromise. But to turn Masonry aside from its high tradition, and make of it a militant order to meddle in politics, is to invite disaster, alienating thousands of thoughtful men from its altar, and defeating the very end for which it exists. Let us never forget the wise words of Emerson, that "the largest is always the truest sentiment," and that we can only overcome evil with good.

Instead, let us renew our vows of loyalty to the great and far shining principles of Freemasonry, and invoke its spirit to descend upon us anew, trusting the lower of Truth, the worth of Character, and the wisdom of Love. Any other course means ruin which God forfend making of Masonry only one more factor in the world of factional feud, an indistinguishable atom in a mass of sectarian and partisan agglomeration. The future of our Fraternity lies in a return to the faith of its fathers, in so far as we have departed from it; bringing the wisdom of the past to the service of the present; teaching the truth that makes men free, "with malice toward none, with charity for all"; showing in the quality of our private lives and public service what Masonry means and the kind of citizens it produces; in short, to make of Masonry today, on a large scale, what in former times it was on a small scale, an order of men initiated, sworn, and trained to make liberty, justice, sweet reasonableness and brotherly love prevail. There may be those who will think this a lame and impotent ending of an argument, to say nothing of a prophecy; but a longer pondering will show them, if they be wise, that the things which made Masonry great in days agone are the things which will make it greater in the future.

Stronger than steel
Is the sword of the Spirit;
Swifter than arrows
The light of the truth is,
Greater than anger
Is love, and subdueth.
Nor is the night starless;
Love is eternal!
God is still God, and
His faith shall not fail us,
Truth is eternal!

For the rest, ye editor does not believe in the infallibility of any man, not even in his own, and he may be in part or altogether wrong in what he has here set down. If so, he begs to be put to rights by his Brethren, and will listen to all they may have it in their hearts to say. Indeed, he invites a thorough discussion of the question, what is to be the future of Freemasonry? It must be much in the minds of thoughtful Masons today, living as we are in a time of upheaval, of questionings many and uncertainties not a few; the more so because, as a fact, we are answering the question whether we know it or not, making today the Masonry of tomorrow! Since the future will have nothing in it save what we bring to it and put into it, surely it behooves us to bethink ourselves betimes, never forgetting the words of the wise poet:

"*Keep the young generations in hail,*
Bequeath to them no tumbled house!"

WAR AND THE MYSTIC TIE

ALAS! it seems decreed that the nations must at last make a desolation, and call it Peace. Anything may happen in these wild and fateful days in which we live, when the whole world is half mad and half of it wholly mad. Many things fair and fine have already been crushed by racial rancors and national hatreds running riot in a vast eruption of savagery, and the end is not yet. Dreadful days lie ahead of us, when the very existence of civilization will hang in the balance, and nothing will be heard but the thunder of great guns and the hot steps of the Lords of Hell as they ride to ruin nothing, save a wail of woe following the evening sun around the world!

Much of what we call modern thought passed quietly away into sleep at midnight on August 4th, 1914, and the Clock of Time was set back for an age. Since that dark date, tie after tie by which men were bound together, has been broken, until little is left but the Law of the Jungle that he may take who has the power and he may keep who can. Science turned traitor, and by its very skill in the mastery of force has changed the beautiful earth into a human slaughter-house. The Church failed, having lost what it claimed to possess, the power to uplift and guide the nations, to draw men to each other, and to base human life on love of man for his fellow. Socialism, with its vague humanitarian mysticism and its fine rhetoric of a cosmopolitan philosophy, collapsed like a house of cards in a storm.

Last of all, the mystic tie of Masonry seems to have given way under the pressure of world-war; the Grand Lodge of England, after a memorable debate, having severed relations with its Teutonic Brethren the Masons of Germany having already repudiated their Brethren in

England, France, and Italy. No doubt it was inevitable that men should act so, looking at each other, as they do, across a million graves where sleep the fathers of dream-children never to be born! We do not chide, we only grieve. Nor do we let go of faith, as not a few have done, for the cynical dogma that humanity, so far from being the offspring of God, was begotten by the Father of Lies, upon the daughter of a Thief its culture a veneer covering an immobile animalism which nothing can alter or influence.

No, no! Albeit we do recall that during the blood and fire and tears of our own Civil War, when States were divided and Churches were rent asunder, the Masonic tie was not broken. While it could not avert the tragedy of war, it did mitigate the horror of it, building rainbow bridges across the battle lines, and many a man in Gray planted a Sprig of Acacia on the grave of a Brother in Blue. Today, those graves where heroes sleep together have sunk level with the sod, and the men who met as foes at Gettysburg have tented together as friends, each paying tribute to the valor of the other. From this fact let us take hope that, no matter how virulent and violent the present war may be, this, too, shall pass away, and the hatred which glows like a furnace today will give place to thoughts of gentleness and pity.

Have no doubt; the men in arms across the sea are not different from us. Soon they will have their Decoration Days, and over the graves of their uncomplaining dead will be drawn closer together, seeing with eyes purified by suffering that the truth which each fought for was but a fragment, a gleam, of a greater truth, and that courage, sacrifice and heroic aspiration are the virtues of all peoples. Men who are now enemies will see each other as they are, and then they will be enemies no more, but friends, even as our North and South, once arrayed in long lines of blue and gray, are now united and free. The Great War will purge the bitterness of spirit from the peoples and a common sorrow will fall upon them like a benediction, the while they turn their energies to the up building of the civilization which their conflict threatened to destroy.

THE BIBLE IN MASONRY

BROTHER Toastmaster: Time is a river and books are boats. Many volumes start down that stream, only to be wrecked and lost beyond recall in its sands. Only a few, a very few, endure the testing's of time and live to bless the ages following. Tonight, we are met to pay homage to the greatest of all books the one enduring Book which has traveled down to us from the far past, freighted with the richest treasure that ever any book has brought to humanity. What a sight it is to see five hundred men gathered about an open Bible how typical of the spirit and genius of Masonry, it's great and simple faith and its benign ministry to mankind.

No Mason needs to be told what a place of honor the Bible has in Masonry. One of the great Lights of the Order, it lies open upon the altar at the center of the lodge. Upon it every Mason takes solemn vows of love, of loyalty, of chastity, of charity, pledging himself to our tenets of Brotherly Love, Relief, and Truth. Think what it means for a young man to make such a covenant of consecration in the morning of life, taking that wise old Book as his guide, teacher and friend! Then as he moves forward from one degree to another, the imagery of the Bible becomes familiar and eloquent, and its mellow, haunting music sings its way into his heart.

And yet, like everything else in Masonry, the Bible, so rich in symbolism, is itself a symbol that is, a part taken for the whole. It is a sovereign symbol of the Book of Faith, the Will of God as man has learned it in the midst of the years that perpetual revelation of Himself which God is making mankind in every land and every age. Thus, by the very honor which Masonry pays to the Bible, it teaches us to revere every book of faith in which men find help for today and hope for the morrow, joining hands with the man of Islam as he takes oath on the Koran, and with the Hindu as he makes covenant with God upon the book that he loves best.

For Masonry knows, what so many forget, that religions are many, but Religion is one perhaps we may say one thing, but that one thing includes everything the life of God in the soul of man, and the duty and hope of man which proceed from His essential character. Therefore, it invites to its altar men of all faiths, knowing that, if they use different names for "the Nameless One of a hundred names," they are yet praying to the one God and Father of all; knowing, also, that while they read different volumes, they are in fact reading the same vast Book of the Faith of Man as revealed in the struggle and sorrow of the race in its quest of God. So that, great and noble as the Bible is, Masonry sees it as a symbol of that eternal Book of the Will of God which Lowell described when he wrote his memorable lines:

> "Slowly the Bible of the race is writ,
>
> And not on paper leaves nor leaves of stone;
>
> Each age, each kindred; adds a verse to it,
>
> Texts of despair or hope, of joy or moan.
>
> While swings the sea, while mists the mountain shroud,
>
> While thunder's surges burst on cliffs of cloud,
>
> Still at the prophets' feet the nations sit."

None the less, much as we honor every book of faith in which any man has found courage to lift his hand above the night that covers him and lay hold of the mighty Hand of God, with us the Bible is supreme What Homer was to the Greeks, what the Koran is to the Arabs, that, and much more, the grand old Bible is to us. It is the mother in our literary family, and if some of its children have grown up and become wise in their own conceit, they yet rejoice to gather about its knee and pay tribute. Not only was the Bible the loom on which our language was woven, but it is a pervasive, refining, redeeming force bequeathed to us, with whatsoever else that is good and true, in the very fiber of our being. Not for a day do we regard the Bible simply as a literary classic, apart from what it means to the faiths and hopes and prayers of men, and it's in weaving into the intellectual and spiritual life of our race.

There was a time when the Bible formed almost the only literature of England; and today, if it were taken away, that literature would be torn to tatters and shreds. Truly did Macaulay say that, if everything else in our language should perish, the Bible would alone suffice to show the whole range and power and beauty of our speech. From it Milton learned his majesty of song, and Ruskin his magic of prose. Carlyle had in his very blood, almost without knowing it, the rhapsody and passion of the prophets their sense of the Infinite, of the littleness of man, of the sarcasm of providence; as Burns, before him, had learned from the same fireside Book the indestructibleness of honor and the humane pity of God which throbbed in his lyrics of love and liberty. Thus, from Shakespeare to Tennyson, the Bible sings in our poetry, chants in our music, echoes in our eloquence, and in our tragedy flashes forever its truth of the terribleness of sin, the tenderness of God, and the inextinguishable hope of man.

My brethren, here is a Book whose scene is the sky and the dirt and all that lies between a Book that has in it the arch of the heavens, the curve of the earth, the ebb and flow of the sea, sunrise and sunset, the peaks of mountains and the glint of sunlight on flowing waters, the shadow of forests on the hills, the song of birds and the color of flowers. But its two great characters are God and the Soul, and the story of their eternal life together is its one everlasting romance. It is the most human of books, telling the old forgotten secrets of the heart, its bitter pessimism and its death-defying hope, its pain, its passion, its sin, its sob of grief and its shout of joy-telling all, without malice, in its Grand Style which can do no wrong, while echoing the sweet-toned pathos of the pity and mercy of God. No other book is so honest with us, so mercilessly merciful, so austere yet so tender, piercing the heart, yet healing the deep wounds of sin and sorrow.

Take this great and simple Book, white with age yet new with the dew of each new morning, tested by the sorrowful and victorious experience of centuries, rich in memories and wet with the tears of multitudes who walked this way before us lay it to heart, love it, read it, and learn what life is, what it means to be a man; aye, learn that God hath made us for Himself, and unquiet are our hearts till they rest in Him. Make it your friend and teacher, and you will know what Sir Walter Scott meant when, as he lay dying, he asked Lockhart to read to him. "From what book?" asked Lockhart, and Scott replied, "There is but one Book!"

THE HOUSE OF THE TEMPLE

WITH ceremonies solemn and impressive, yet simple in spirit and eloquent in form, the new House of the Temple was dedicated in Washington city, October 18th, the home of the Ancient and Accepted Scottish Rite in its Southern Jurisdiction. It was a lovely day, and more than five thousand people, including distinguished Masons from all over the country, witnessed the consecration of one of the most unique and imposing buildings on this continent at once a monument to the founders of the Order and an emblem of the influence and power of the Rite. As the Grand Prior sprinkled the oil, consecrating the Temple to "Mutual Concession, Charitable Judgment, and Toleration," a White Dove flew from across the street, entered the building, then returned to the bright sunlight amid the acclaim of the assembly who interpreted it as a token in accord with the Spirit of Masonry and the eternal fitness of things.

Our Frontispiece shows the House of the Temple from the outside, and the accompanying illustrations disclose two of its stately chambers; but to describe such a building in a few words is too daring a thing to attempt. Truly, it is Freemasonry carved in stone; a great Symbol in itself, epitomizing by virtue of its Simplicity in Magnificence, its Grandeur and Beauty of conception, the Faith, the Philosophy, the Genius and the Prophecy of the Order cemented here, once for all, in a noble emblem destined to withstand the storms of time and the mutations of human torture. In design it is a Square crowned by a Triangle, approached by Three, Five, Seven and Nine steps, its gate guarded by a Sphinx on either side, bespeaking the Wisdom and Power of God; and so it will stand as one generation cometh and another generation goeth, a mute but eloquent witness of the truth that, if Man would build for Eternity, he must imitate on earth the House not made with hands. With right was it dedicated

"To Purity, Innocence of Act, Word, and Thought; to Mutual Concession, Charitable Judgment, and Toleration; to Charity, Compassion, and Sympathy; to Justice, Night, and Truth; to Universal Benevolence and Good Will Towards Men; to Wise Legislation, Good Faith, Stainless Loyalty, and Honor; a Symbol of Gratitude, Veneration, and Love of God, and a pledge of Future Fidelity and Performance of Duty.

Masons of every land, of every Rite, will join in the words of the Sovereign Grand Commander, grave words fitly spoken in which Prayer is blended with Prophecy, and Aspiration with Resolution, when he said:

"May guile and deceit, false pretense and hypocrisy never intrude within these doors; but let there always stand as vigilant tilers, sincerity and frankness, plain dealing and earnestness to forbid the approach of any unclean visitor. For the increase of loving kindness, which is the soul of all religion, to be the shrine of honor and duty, inseparable as the Dioscuri; for the glorifying and magnifying of truth, which, sown in whatever barren and rocky soil, springs up and yields a hundredfold for use and blessing; for the conquest everywhere of the hydra of tolerance, hatred and persecution; for toleration to which Masonry erects its altars, garlanded with flowers; and to aid in establishing everywhere the dominion of God and faith in human nature, of hope, the chief blessing bestowed by Providence on man, and of charity, divinest of all the virtues, this House of the Temple has been consecrated."

THE PATRIARCHS

MR. TOASTMASTER: Surely the idea of such an evening as this was most happy. There is a day set apart in honor of our mothers, God bless them! and no one would detract one iota from its sanctity and beauty. But it has remained for this lodge to dedicate a day to our fathers, and especially to the fathers of Masonry into whose labors we have entered, and of whose prophetic sowing we are reaping the harvest. Of truth, we honor ourselves when we meet and pay tribute to men who did so much to make Masonry what it is.

Some do not well know that there was a time, and not so long ago, when it was a courageous thing for a man to be a Mason. Prejudice against the order was intense, often fanatical, and our gentle craft was held by many to be a dangerous fraternity, as if its innocent secrets harbored dark designs. How different it is now. Today our order is everywhere honored, and our gates are thronged with young men eager to enter its ancient fellowship. What has brought about this change of feeling and attitude toward Masonry? More than all else, it is due to the quiet dignity of the men of the order, and the noble way in which they have shown what Masonry is in their lives. Nearly every man here, if asked directly, would admit that he was drawn to Masonry by the quality of its men. After all, the greatest influence of Masonry in the world, is the silent, eloquent influence of character.

A FEW OLD BRETHREN

It may be interesting to some to know that such an evening as this recalls one of the oldest traditions of the order. If you will look into the "Old Charges" the title deeds of Masonry, and a part of its earliest ritual you will see that among the duties required of a young man entering the order, was that he respect the aged. When, after a period of decline, the Grand Lodge of England was organized in 1717, who presided over the assembly? In the scanty records of that scene, it is set down as significant that the Grand Lodge came to order with "the oldest Master Mason in the chair." Indeed, it seems clear that the impulse by which the scattered Masons of the time were drawn together into closer union, came, as Anderson suggests, from "a few old brethren"; and during the critical period of transition, it was the old men who guided the craft. For the first Grand Lodge, so far from being an innovation, was in fact a revival of the old quarterly Assembly, and was intended to preserve the ancient usages of the order. So that, our meeting this night in honor of the veterans of the craft, has the sanction, not only of our own finer feeling for the fitness of things, but of the long tradition and custom of the order.

When is a man old? Age is said to be a matter of feeling, not of years, but old age seemed to come upon men earlier in former times than it does now. At the age of 49 Shakespeare sold his holdings in the London theatres, retired from active life, and went back to Stratford. Dr. Johnson felt himself old at 40, and Lincoln at the age of 48 spoke of himself as old and withered. The Roman senate was an assembly of old men, but there was a law that no senator over 60 should be called to his duties, lest his failing mind bring harm to the republic. But it is different with us today. With us, a man is intellectually in his prime at 60, and many do their best work much later. Gladstone, at 70, was just entering the second volume of his biography.

YOUNG OLD MEN

When is a man a patriarch? Let me tell you. Old age is that period when one sees the limit of life, whether it be at 20, 50, or 80; when he sees clearly, what once was covered by mists, a grave full of songs unsung, hopes unrealized, and ambitions unachieved. There are men, not yet 30, who are asking that ultimate question: "What is the use?" These are the old men, old of heart, world-weary, smitten with palsy of soul, and gray with a sense of futility; these are the unburied dead. Think of a man asking such a question in a world where sunsets are like sacraments, and the hush and solemnity of the dawn is like the smile of God! Think of finding life flat, stale and unprofitable in a world where the incredible is an everyday fact, and the impossible is always coming true a world where there is truth to seek, love to consecrate, and hope forever building its great Arch of Promise! Such a man has come too early to the sear and yellow leaf.

Also, there are men far along in years, walking down the western slope where the shadows lengthen towards evening, who are eager and alert of spirit, happy and forward-looking, their faith undimmed, their zest of life unabated. These are not old men. There is in them a foregleam of the immortal life. Years have piled up betimes, but they have kept their faith firm, their feelings buoyant, their sympathies active, and their interest in life fresh and vivid. How fine it is to see a man grow old reverently and beautifully, his heart aglow with the soft light of eventide and the glory of the star-crowned night! It is not strange that such men enjoy the authority of influence and counsel, wisdom and prophecy, which Cicero held to be the trophies of age.

THE SEVEN AGES OF MAN

Each of the seven ages of men, as Shakespeare marked them, has its uses, its joys, its disadvantages, and its compensations. He is a wise man who takes life as it is, each degree as God confers it, each experience in its season, youth with its flaming visions, age with its serenity. For age is opportunity not less than youth, albeit in another form. Old age, to be sure, has its disadvantages and perils. Failing strength, stiff joints, "the lean and slippered pantaloons, sans teeth, sans eyes, sans taste" these are familiar enough. Often it weakens the tenacity of memory, but if we can manage to forget what is not worth remembering, that might be enviable. With few exceptions like Sophocles and Tennyson age clips the wings of imagination; but it also cools our passion which befogs and pervert's reason. Age is clarifying and may attain, as Milton said, to "something of prophetic strain."

At least, it belongs to age, in a life well spent, to look upon the world with calm and wise vision. As Plato said in his Republic, old age "certainly has a great sense of freedom and serenity"; but he added, "the cause is to be sought, not in the ages of men, but in their tempers and characters." That is to say, it is quality and not the quantity of life that counts for most. The fact that a man has lived on this earth three score years and ten does not mean, necessarily, that he is either good or wise. Some men are as foolish in age as they were in youth. Doubly foolish is he who, living to grow old, has not learned the priceless value of virtue, and the wisdom of love. Time alone brings neither honor nor wisdom.

THE SADDEST THING ON EARTH

An eastern king offered a reward to the one who would tell him the saddest thing on earth. There were three competitors in the contest. One said it is unrequited love; another that it is the death of the young; and the third, who won the prize, that it is old age and poverty. I do not believe it, unless by poverty you mean that pitiful penury of soul which makes the gloaming of life so desolate. No; the saddest thing on this earth is old age and sin, an old man crass, crafty, hard, cynical, and impure! Great God! rather than come to such an end, let me die tonight, in the morning of life, my work hardly begun!

When we are young, we draw checks on the Bank of the Future. Some men go on doing this, unable, it seems, to live year in and year out upon their current income. Not many of those checks are cashed at full value. There is nearly always a heavy discount, and more often they come back to us for lack of funds. When we are old, we draw our checks on the Bank of the Past. Whether they are cashed or not depends on how thrifty we have been in laying up that treasure which neither moth nor rust can corrupt, nor thieves break through and steal. More precious than rubies is a wise faith purified by trial, a conscience void of offense, and the memory of years spent in purity, honor and service. When a man comes to the end, the only things he does not regret, and would not recall if he could, are the kind words spoken and the deeds done in love of God and his fellow men. At that hour an empty alabaster box, with which he has anointed some friend in need, counts for more than all the gold in all the hills!

YOUTH AND AGE

Other things being equal, the advantages of age, though less obvious, far outweigh its handicaps. For one thing, age sees life in a long perspective and in a clearer, if drier, light. It has a vision of the beauty and grace and folly of youth, which youth does not have. It is the young who despise youth and try to get away from it, the urchin longing to be a schoolboy, the freshman to be a senior. No man, when a boy, ever had half the joy running across the meadow that he gets from seeing his boy, not to say his grandson, on that very spot. It is the old who see the loveliness of youth, and love it. Youth is the drama, in which the actors are absorbed in their parts; age is the audience. By virtue of its detachment, age has a truer insight into life, and if it knows little of ecstasy it knows less of despair.

With the mellowing of life, there comes also a deeper sense of the kinship of things. Youth loves cliques, the more exclusive the better; it rarely gives love unless it is returned. Not so age, whose affections, if less turbulent, are less touched by selfish motives. Age makes little of human differences, and sets much store by the great common fellowship of humanity, seeing many ties of union where youth sees only discord. Work, too, takes on a new aspect with lengthening years. Old men do not feel, as young men often do, that the universe rests upon their shoulders. Nor do they imagine, as Hamlet did, that they were born to set the world right. They see that each must be content to do his little human part, and trust the fate of the world to a Power greater than man. If age limits a man, it the better sets his bounds within which he can work quietly, and get something done before he dies.

HAMLET AND PROSPERO

Youth seeks very high for what age finds nearby. It is when we grow older that the simple things of life begin to unfold their wonder, and open long vistas of meditation. Nogi fought great battles on the plains of Manchuria, but towards the end he was wont to muse over an iris, finding in its beauty a mystery beyond his fathoming. Youth knows more than old age, because it knows so many things that are not so. After 50, our bottle of knowledge is so shaken that it is all of one color. When we are young, we love Hamlet, with his obscure, haunting melancholy, but when age comes on we like best the wisdom of Prospero who, by the aid of Ariel, won victory over Caliban. Age may not be more religious than youth, but it is religious in a different and deeper way. It thinks of God, not as a flaming fire, but as an abiding presence, made real by the revealing's of the years serene, infinitely patient, unutterably great and kind. Youth is for faith; old age for trust.

Why did Shakespeare all at once drop his task and go back to Stratford? No doubt many things blended in the making of the decision, one of which was that he was wise enough to know when to quit. Another fact may have been the elemental love of man for the earth, his great mother, in whose bosom he sleeps at last. But perhaps the chief motive was a desire for quiet amid the scenes of his boyhood, and time to gather the threads of his thought and weave them into a fabric of faith. There is a deep instinct which leads a man back to his native place, as many of you have made long journeys to Ohio, New York, or Maine just to see the sun come up over the hill or sea. One finds something homelike in his native landscape, and in the old haunts a man can fuse his latest thought with his earliest memory as he can hardly do anywhere else. Some such feeling must have led Shakespeare to leave London and go back to the winding Avon. And it was there that he wrote the gentlest of all his plays, the Tempest a miracle of art, an allegory of the victory of man over fate and fortune by self-surrender to the highest laws of life.

THE HOUSE OF FAITH

Similarly, Albert Pike used to urge upon old men the study of Masonry, not only because it brings to us from afar the high and simple wisdom of humanity, but it offers to every man a great hope and consolation. At its altar a man may gather up his deepest thoughts which, in the busy mid-years of life, are too often left scattered in the disarray of a temple yet unbuilt, and fashion them into a House of Faith a Home of the Soul. How to live is the one matter; and the oldest man in his ripe age has never found a wiser way than to build, year by year, on a foundation of faith in God and love of man, using the Square to test the rightness of our lives, the Plumb line to mark the rectitude of our acts, the Compasses to keep our passions within bounds, and the Rule to divide our days into labor, rest and service. Love is ever the Builder, and whoso obeys its sweet law and builds after its pattern will not be left shelterless and alone.

After old age, what? Ever the evening shadows fall; ever there comes a time, to whomsoever is a man, when even the wisest knows not where he is; ever and ever the twilight and after that the dark, when all the lights of philosophy go out, and only faith and hope and love remain. There is nothing for it but to walk calmly down the western slope, the sun shining in our faces, into the evening shadows trusting the great God over all.

"Grow old along with me!
The best is yet to be,
The last of life

For which the first was made;
Our times are in his hands
Who sayeth, 'A whole I planned,
Youth shows but half; trust God;
See all, nor be afraid.' "

Bede the Venerable, in giving an account of the deliberations of the King of Northumberland and his counsellors, as to whether they should allow the Christian missionaries to teach a new faith to the people, recites this eloquent incident. After much debate, a grey-haired chief stood up and spoke, recalling the feeling that came over him on seeing a little bird pass through, on fluttering wing, the warm bright hall of feasting, while the winter winds raged without. The moment of its flight was full of sweetness and light for the bird, but it was brief. Out of the darkness it flew, looked upon the gay scene, and vanished into the darkness, none knowing whence it came nor whither it went.

"Like this," said the veteran chief, "is human life. We come, our wisest men know not whence. We go, they cannot tell whither. Our flight is brief. Therefore, if there be anyone that can teach us more about it in God's name let us hear him!"

ARTHUR EDWARD WAITE - AN APPRECIATION

ONE of the greatest masters of the field of esoteric lore and method of culture, by far the greatest now living, is Arthur Edward Waite, to whom it is an honor to pay tribute. In response to a number of requests, and as prelude to a lecture on the deeper aspects of Masonry, soon to appear in these pages, we offer a brief sketch of Brother Waite, with a statement of his conception of Masonry and its service to man in his quest of God. If these lines induce any of our readers to study his works, they will thank us for having put them in the way of so wise and skillful a guide, who is at once a poet and a mystic, the sum of whose insight, set forth on his latest page, is that;

"All thoughts, all passions, all delights, Whatever stirs this mortal frame, Are but the ministers of love, And feed his sacred flame."

By rare good fortune, as we think, our friend and teacher was born in America in Brooklyn, New York and on his father's side traces his descent back to the earliest settlers in Connecticut. His mother was English, belonging to the old family of Lovell. The family name, originally spelled "Wayte," was attached to the document authorizing the execution of Charles I, and it was probably the fact that the family found England a rather uncomfortable place in which to live after the Restoration that sent his ancestors across the sea. While the poet was still in his infancy, his father died, and he was taken to England at the age of two. He has never returned to

America a fact to be held against him, but for which we hope he will atone in a time not far away.

Educated privately, he began writing while still in his early teens, poetry being his first love. His first book, a volume of verse, was published in 1886. For ten years or more he pursued an active business life, as secretary and director of public companies, at the same time engaging in elaborate researches in the fields of magic, occultism, and the esoteric side of religion and philosophy. How he found time to do both is not easy to know. He took the whole realm of mysticism for his province, for the study of which he was almost ideally fitted by temperament, training, and genius and, we may add, by certain deep experiences in his own life, of which he rarely speaks, the glow of which one detects in all his work, and nowhere more vividly than in his latest book on "The Way of Divine Union." In later years, as the result of long study, he has come to deal only with the higher mysticism, as totally separated from the magical, the psychical, and the occult.

Exploring a hidden world, he has brought to his task a religious nature, the accuracy and skill of a scholar, a sureness and delicacy of insight at once sympathetic and critical, the eye of a symbolist and the soul of a poet-qualities rarely found in union. Brother Waite does not write after our American fashion "hot off the bat," as Casey put it but in a leisurely manner, seeking not only to state the results of his research, but to convey somewhat of the atmosphere of the themes with which he deals. Prolific but seldom prolix, he writes with such lucidity as his subject admits of, albeit in a style often touched with strange lights and remote and haunting echoes. Much learning and many kinds of wisdom are in his pages; and if he is of those who turn down another street when wonders are wrought in the neighborhood, it is because, having found the inner truth, he does not ask for a sign.

Always our Brother writes in the conviction that all great subjects bring us back to the one subject that is alone great the attainment of that Living Truth which is about us everywhere. He conceives of our human life as one eternal Quest of that Living Truth, taking many forms, yet ever at heart the same aspiration, to trace which he has made it his labor and reward. Through all his pages he is following the tradition of this Quest, in its myriad aspects, finding in it the secret meaning of the life of man from his birth to his union or reunion with God who is his Goal. And the result is a series of volumes noble in form! united in aim, unique in wealth of revealing beauty, of exquisite insight, and of unequalled worth.

As far back as 1886, Brother Waite issued his study of the "Mysteries of Magic," a digest of the writings of Eliphas Levi, to whom Albert Pike was more indebted than he let us know. Then followed the "Real History of the Rosicrucian's," which traces, as far as such a thing can be done, the thread of fact in that fascinating romance. Of the Quest in its distinctively Christian aspect, he has written in "The Hidden Church of the Holy Grail"; a work of rare beauty, of bewildering richness, its style partaking of the story told, and not at all after the fashion of these days. But the Graal Legend is only one aspect of the old-world sacred Quest of the truth most worth finding, uniting the symbols of chivalry with the forms of Christian faith.

Masonry is another aspect of that same age-long Quest; and just as Brother Pound has shown us the place of Masonry among the institutions of humanity, and its meaning as such, so Brother Waite shows us the place of Masonry in the mystical tradition and aspiration of mankind. No one may ever hope to write of "The Secret Tradition in Masonry" with more insight and charm, or a touch more sure and revealing, than this gracious scholar to whom Masonry perpetuates the Instituted Mysteries of antiquity, with much else derived from innumerable store houses of treasure. What then are the marks of this eternal Quest, whether its legend be woven about a Lost Word, a design left unfinished by a Master Builder, or, in its Christian form, about the Cup of Christ?

They are as follows: first, the sense of a great loss which has befallen humanity, making us a race of pilgrims ever in search of that which is lost; second, the intimation that what was lost still exists somewhere in time and the world, although deeply buried; third, the faith that it will ultimately be found and the vanished glory restored; fourth, the substitution of something temporary and less than the best, but never in a way to adjourn the quest; and fifth, the felt presence of that which is lost under veils and symbols close at hand. What though it takes many forms, it is always the same quest, and from this statement of it surely we ought to see that Masonry has a place in the greatest quest which man has pursued in the midst of time. Our Order is thus linked with the shining tradition of the race, having a place and a service in the culture of the life of the soul, leading men in the search for God, if haply they might feel after Him, and find Him, though He is not far from any one of us.

But this is a long and difficult quest, and we must walk carefully, lest we trip and fall into the pits that beset the path. Brother Waite warns us against the dark alleys that lead nowhere, and the false lights that lure to ruin, and he protests against those who would open the Pandora's Box of the Occult on the altar of Masonry. After a long study of occultism, magic, omens, talismans, and the like, he has come to draw a sharp line between the occult and the mystical, and therein he is wise. From a recent interview with him in regard to these matters in an English paper, we may read:

"There is nothing more completely set apart from mysticism than that set of interests and things called occultism. Occultism is concerned with the idea that there were a number of secret sciences handed down from the past, and which, roughly speaking, represented the steps toward the attainment of abnormal power by man, corresponding to the idea of Magic. Magic, of course, meant many things: it meant the power obtained by man as a result of dealing with spirits, raising the spirits of the dead, everything that we understand by the supposed efficacy of talismans, and all that is comprehended in the word Astrology. My interest in these things has been purely historical and critical.

Occult and psychical research does help, of course, to show that the purely materialistic interpretation of things does not cover the whole field. It shows a residue of experience which points to the existent of powers beyond the ken of man, some of them maleficent, others innocent in themselves, of which the student may take account. Unfortunately, I have known too many who follow these things as the be-all and end-all of their interests. I know others also, and many, to whom the exaggerated pursuit has spelt not less than ruin. I mean, morally and spiritually. I know, for the rest, that they reach no real term; very soon they come up against a dead wall."

Here are grave and wise words, spoken out of full knowledge of history and fact, and he is wise who heeds them. It is no theological bias of any sort, but the profound fallacy of the occult, and its danger to the highest life and character, that has moved us more than once in these pages to utter a like warning to those who would turn aside from the historic highway of the soul to follow a will-of-the-wisp into the bog. If Masonry forsakes its Great Light to follow these wandering tapers, it too will fall into the ditch. But to listen to Brother Waite:

"Symbolism is sacramental. To me, all visible things are emblems. When you come to think of it, is it not true that all the workings of the human mind are in the form of symbols? These symbols are truly representative and not mere figments of the mind, and to get at the reality behind the symbol is the aim of the mystic. The theory of mysticism is that the voice of God is within, and that the soul has to enter into the realization that God is within. The question is whether that realization can be fully achieved in this life. All, or nearly all, the great mystics, held that they only approximated it. The absolute vision and union lie very far away, so the quest of the Lost Word goes on, ever on.

Mysticism is not a way of escape either from one's self or the world. It is by the realization of the indwelling of God in all around, and within, in things animate and inanimate, and most of all in the soul of man, that we attain to knowledge of Godin so far as we attain it in this life. Thus, it is not a path of escape from the world, as the old ascetics imagine, but by finding God in the world, the ideal in the real, one with the ideal within ourselves, that we attain to union with God. We are sacraments to ourselves. A man building a house would perhaps be surprised if you told him that he is not merely building bricks and stones, but that he is trying to bring into being something of the idealism in his own nature, but if he could be brought to understand that, would it not give a new glory to his work?"

Thus, mysticism, as here presented, is practical common sense, bringing to the humblest task the highest truth to lighten and transfigure our labor. Time does not permit us to speak of the poetry of Brother Waite, though some think his best work has been done in that field. He himself thinks of his poetry as "light tongued rumors and hints alone of the songs I had hoped to sing." We must, however, mention his drama of "The Morality of the Lost

Word," which may be found in his poems, recently collected in two noble volumes, and we bespeak for it a long study. At another time we shall speak of the poetry of our friend to whom the world is ever an infinite parable, giving at present only the following lines as a hint of his poetic purpose and power:

In the midst of a world full of omen and sign, impell'd by the seeing gift On auspice and portent reflecting, in part I conjecture their drift; I catch faint words of the language which the world speaks far and wide. And the soul withdrawn in the deeps of man from the birth of each man has cried. I know that a sense is beyond the sense of the manifest Voice and Word, That the tones in the chant which we strain to seize are the tones that are scarcely heard; While life pulsating with secret things has many too deep to speak, And that which evades, with a quailing heart, we feel is the sense we seek: Scant were the skill to discern a few where the countless symbols crowd, To render the easiest reading, catch the cry that is trite and loud.

For the rest, we confess a great debt to our dear friend and Brother across the great waters, divided by distance but very near in thought and sympathy and regard; a man of pure and lofty spirit, tolerant of mind, noble of nature, in all ways a true Master Mason and one who does not forget "that best portion of a good man's life, the little, nameless, unremembered acts of kindness and of love."

EDWIN MARKHAM - POET OF BROTHERHOOD

AMONG the poets of America now living there is none greater, alike in personal character and wealth of genius, than Edwin Markham, who is the noblest Masonic singer since Robert Burns. Sweet of heart, with a mind full of benign light, he sings of the old simplicities and sanctities which must lie at the basis of individual worth and social welfare, the while he teaches us to see and to follow "that thread of all sustaining Beauty that runs through all and doth all unite." He is, indeed, the supreme poet, since Whitman, of the goodly, gracious gospel of Brotherly Love so much needed in the world now and always. Here follows a brief sketch of the man, with an appreciation of his genius as a singer and a seer.

There is nothing for surprise that such a man descends from a sturdy ancestry, both intellectual and moral. On his paternal side, his lineage runs back to Colonel Markham, the first cousin and secretary of William Penn, and later acting governor of Pennsylvania. His maternal line, through the Winchell's, runs back into the best stock of New and Old England and Holland. Our poet was born in Oregon, in 1852, whither his pioneer parents had moved from Michigan. His father dying when the boy was little more than four years of age, we find him living with his mother and brother in one of the remote romantic valleys of California. His mother was a woman of rather silent nature, his brother was deaf and dumb, and the lad was left much alone with nature and his own inner life. Years of quiet brooding, while he followed the cattle or folded the sheep, developed depth and originality of mind, evoking the poet soul within him. Memories of those days when he was a shepherd boy find echo in his poems, as, for example, in "The Heart's Return."

Partly, at least, his gift of song was an inheritance, for his mother, albeit so quiet and reserved, was a lover of poetry and a writer of verse on her own account. Some of her lines were frequently to be found in the papers of the time. The first money that Edwin earned was twenty-five dollars for ploughing a neighbor's field, which his mother told him was his, and that he might have whatever he wished to buy with it. He bought books Webster's Unabridged Dictionary, and the poems of Tennyson, Bryant and Moore. It is not difficult to imagine the use to which he put those precious volumes in the leisure that was his in the peaceful valley of Suisun, where he tended the flocks and herds. His chance for early technical training was slight about three months in the year, and not always that, but he studied diligently, making the best use of whatever books came his way. Also, he worked and dreamed and laid plans, in such various ways as ambitious boys can devise, until at eighteen he entered the State Normal School at San Jose, and later finished his schoolwork at Christian College, Santa Rosa. Believing in the value of handicraft, he mastered the secrets of blacksmithing, and wrought at the forge for a time. But a man of his genius was not allowed to remain at the forge, and he was soon called to other and higher service.

Markham was made a Mason in Acacia Lodge No. 92, at Coloma, California, in the early eighties, and he has an abiding interest in the Order. From the first the Spirit of Masonry moved him deeply, as was natural for a man to whom Brotherhood is not only "the crest and crowning of all good," but religion in its deeper name, and who sees that,

"The fine audacities of honest deed,

The homely old integrities of soul,"

must be the foundation alike of personal character and social beauty. He reckons Masonry among the deep, quiet, beautiful forces destined to soften the hard winter of the world into a great summertime of friendship and goodwill. Of one who is so chaste of soul, so aglow with the joy of life and the wonder of the world, and so brotherly withal, it may be said that he has found the Master's Word. His friend Joaquin Miller said of him years ago:

"Markham has always seemed to me the purest of the pure; the cleanest minded man of all the many great and good of his high calling I have known, and it has been my high privilege to know nearly all of the great authors of Saxon lands this last third of a century."

With Markham poetry is not a byplay, nor a soft sensuous sentimentality, but a high and heavenly vocation, the fit vehicle for the expression of the truths that make us men. There is something of the urge of divine necessity in all his song, and a sense of consecration. It is the prophetic element that one feels in his music, as of a man who has heard unutterable things and must speak. One cannot read "The Whirlwind Road," for instance, without being reminded of St. Paul and the company of those who live the dedicated life. For him, the home of the poet is on the heights, and his mission is one of leadership no "idle singer of an empty day," but a pilot voice foretelling a new day:

"Life is a mission stern as fate,
And song a dread apostolate.

The toils of prophecy are his,
To hail the coming centuries,
To ease the steps and lift the load
Of souls that falter on the road.
He presses on before the race,
And sings out of a silent place,
And the dim path he breaks today
Will sometime be a trodden way."

Resolutely, he has held himself true to this high ideal of his art, refining his gold and bringing to it every test, and few men of our day have more to tell us. Back of all the poetry of Markham lies a grand philosophy which sees that the great Soul of the World is just, and loving too. For him, the import of life is deep, deeper than time and the grave, and an awful but judicial Spirit moves behind our human scene, weighing the stars, weighing the deeds of men. He is a hushed worshipper before that high benignant Spirit that goes untarrying to the reckoning hour, defeating the injustices of men. As we may read in the poem on Dreyfus:

"*O men that forge the fetter, it is vain;*
There is a Still Hand stronger than you chain.
'Tis no avail to bargain, sneer and nod,
And shrug the shoulder for reply to God.

From the mighty hand of God so still, yet so sure these is no escape, here or hereafter or anywhere. How compellingly, yet how compassionately, he teaches this truth in many a golden song. Since George Eliot there has arisen no more strenuous apostle of the human deed than Markham. Insistently, consistently, eloquently, he teaches the absolute justice that lies at the root of things, and the righteousness to which men must bow at last. Take, for example, his lines to "The Suicide." How few the words, how vast the significance! It is a whole philosophy with one dip of the pen:

"Toil-worn, and trusting Zeno's mad belief,

A soul went wailing from the world of grief;

A wild hope led the way,

Then suddenly dismay!

So the old load was there,

The duty, the despair!

Nothing had changed; still only one escape

From its old self into the angel shape."

No escape in life or death, save in obedience to the just and loving will of God. What is the will of God? What, indeed, as our own hearts tell us, but that we must be pure of heart and brotherly of spirit, making our daily bread "brother-bread," and living to serve our fellow souls? Markham has written of Religion as the Art of Life, and of poetry as the Soul of Religion as witness his exquisite study of "The Poetry of Jesus." But, profoundly religious as he is, religion means for him personal chastity and human ministry, brotherliness of spirit and deed. Therefore, he bids us pray in words, but also, and still more, in works, for purity of soul, for loving fidelity to one another, for freedom and fellowship among men.

Like all the wise ones of old, our poet holds that we know as much as we do. Friar Hilary, in "The Hindered Quest," inured in his cell, sought peace in vain till, hearing a cry of human need, he went forth to do a kindly deed; then, as the Master told him,

"You turned at last your rusty key
And left the door ajar for Me,"

which states in a thumbnail space enough for a creed and a dozen commentaries. So also in "The Angelus," that collect for any day in the week, and for every month in the year; and also in "The Father's Business," to name two of many poems. To the old, brutal question of Cain, Am I my brother's keeper? Markham makes reply that we are born for the practice of the Golden Rule, and our destiny is to learn to live and let live, to think and let think, building a social order that is wise and just and pure.

"There is a destiny that makes us Brothers;
None goes his way alone;
All we send into the lives of others
Comes back into our own."

Indeed, our poet holds that the need of man may be summed up in Bread, Beauty, and Brotherhood-Bread, the symbol of physical necessities which must be met ere man can rise to the higher human life; Beauty, that manna from heaven to feed the hungry soul on its pilgrimage; and Brotherhood, the one prophetic word which describes the translation of the ideal into the real. When we learn to be brotherly, men will not be used to make money, but money will be used to make men. Aye, when we have mastered the fine art of freedom, justice and kindly living, the weary tragedy of human history will become a chant of victory. And until we learn the brotherly life, "we men are slaves and travel downward to the dust of graves." Here is our material; here our tools and our divine design:

> *"We men of earth have here the stuff*
>
> *Of Paradise we have enough!*
>
> *We need no other thing to build*
>
> *The stairs into the Unfulfilled,*
>
> *No other ivory for the doors,*
>
> *No other marble for the floors,*
>
> *No other cedar for the beam*
>
> *And dome of man's immortal dream*
>
> *Here on the paths of every day,*
>
> *Here on the common human way,*
>
> *Is all the busy gods would take*
>
> *To build a heaven, to mold and make*
>
> *New Edens. Ours the stuff sublime*
>
> *To build Eternity in time."*

America, in the vision of Markham, is the last great hope of man, because it offers an opportunity for the practice of Brotherhood. That is its imperious errand among the nations, and "The Need of the Hour," and all hours, is for fearless, faithful leadership of honest and true men "star led to build the world again" such leadership as we had when Lincoln lived. Surely Markham has written the noblest of all poems in praise of Lincoln. There is not another like it anywhere. If he had written nothing else, he would be entitled to our lasting and grateful remembrance. In a wild and fateful hour, when the nation was in dire plight, the Norn-Mother bent the heavens and came down to make a man to match the mortal need:

"She took the tried clay from the common road,

Clay warm yet with the genial heat of earth,

Dashed through it all a strain of prophecy;

Then mixed laughter with the serious stuff.

It was a stuff to wear for centuries,

A man that matched the mountains and compelled

The stars to look our way and honor us."

Truly, he is a "good gray poet" blessings on his head! so gracious to know, so glorious to hear, simple, unaffected, kindly, athrob with faith and hope and love. His last book, "The Shoes of Happiness," is in some ways his best. His message is the same as of yore, but it becomes richer, deeper and more varied in its exposition-sun-bright sonnets, deep-hearted lyrics coming to the aid of stories, parables and quatrains, and Longfellow might envy the exquisite grace of "The Jugglers of Touraine." The group of songs under "The Hero of the Cross," notable alike in insight and art, are reverent, austere, beautiful, and worthy of high rank in the Christian Melody. He is of those who know the way to Emmaus, and the White Comrade who journeys with us when we walk that sunset path. The first lines of this last book are familiar to our readers, but they are too characteristic of the inclusive fellowship of the man and the wise strategy of his love to omit:

"He drew a circle that shut me out,

Heretic, rebel, a thing to flout,

But love and I had the wit to win:

We drew a circle that took him in."

Apollo has been kind to our poet-friend and Brother, granting him in its fullness the prayer of Horace: a sane and healthy old age consoled by sweet song. His idealism has not waned with the years. Time has taught him a deeper faith that forereaches the greater tomorrow that he so surely sees is on the way. It may not come in perfectness in his day, or in ours, but come it will, as morning follows night:

"Come, clear the way, then, clear the way;

Blind creeds and kings have had their day.

Break the dead branches from the path;

Our hope is in the aftermath,

Our hope is in heroic men,

Star-led to build the world again.

To this event the ages ran:

Make way for Brotherhood make way for Man!"

IF A MAN DIE

ONCE again, the white death of Winter gives way to the wonder of Spring, and the heart of man feels the thrill and stir of that flood of life which returns to renew the world. Soon the bare earth and the gaunt, gray hills will be clad in the living green of rustling woods and the glint of laughing waters, as ever it has been in all the ages agone. Time out of mind man has seen in this ancient ritual of Nature a symbol of the life of the Soul, of a dim splendor ever on before, of a victory ever about to be realized, a ray of light piercing "that shadow that keeps the key to all the creeds."

If a man die-aye, there is the rub, since no man knows that any man dies, save only in appearance. Of death, as we use the word and the meaning we give to it, Nature knows nothing: there is simply no such thing. This is not to minify the grave, to which all things mortal decline, as if it were a matter of light import. In nowise. There is something appalling in the masterful negation and collapse of the body, and when Tolstoi describes it, we feel almost as if it had fallen upon us. It is pathetic. It is profound. Yet we may be too easily overawed by its material aspect, and mistake a physical fact for a spiritual tragedy. What avails it what any man may have to say about death? The real question is, what shall we say to it, or shall we let it have the last word?

After all, the chief fact about man is not his body, but his mind with its thoughts that wander through eternity, his soul with its many-winged splendor of aspiration and of hope. Reason, Love, and the Moral Sense these things are of more than time and sense, for, unless we who think of time stand in some way above and apart from it, there could be no such idea. That is to say, if man lives by the law of his higher nature, he must live for things which have their source and satisfaction beyond the borne of Time and Place. In short, man is a being who, if he be not immortal is called by the law of his being to live and act as if he were immortal and he is wise, whatever else may be his folly, in that he dares to trust the prophetic promptings of his nature against the verdict of the senses and the shadow of the grave.

But the real proof of faith lies not in logic, nor in the balancing of probabilities, but in a certain deep and daring kind of living wherein life reveals its own eternal quality. The real answer to all our wistful questionings is to be found in the way of Divine union, being a fact of experience in the inward life, and it were better to be absorbed in the quest of that union than to be ever canvassing the shadowy field of conjecture, tormented, uncertain, and weary of heart. As the soul ascends the Mountain of the Lord its "muddy vesture of decay" becomes less opaque, until at last, by the witness of those who have made the venture and won the victory, assurance is made doubly sure in a fellowship ineffable with Him whom to know aright is Life Eternal. It must be so. Life is unbeginning, and so unending, because life is from God. Let us be content with what is already our own, equally by virtue of Divine heredity and the right of spiritual valor and conquest, "even life forever more" life rich, abundant, radiant, eternal!

ST. JOHN'S DAY

AN old Latin document of our Order, said to be deposited with a Lodge at Namur, and purporting to be a proclamation of the Masons of Europe, assembled at Cologne in 1535, declares that Masons are called "Brethren dedicated to St. John," first among the martyr stars of the morning. It tells us, further, that prior to 1440, the Fraternity was called the Joannite Brethren, but that about that time it began to be known by the name of Freemasons. No doubt it is largely fiction, but it may serve as a text for an inquiry as to the relation of the two Saints John, and especially of St. John the Baptist, to our Order.

There is no proof that either of these holy men were ever patrons of our Fraternity, but it is a fact that Masonry has patronized them for ages. The reason for this may be obscure so far as history is concerned, but it is obvious enough if we have a care for spiritual suggestion and the fitness of things. One was a prophet bearing witness to the Light, the other an evangelist of Love; and since the object of Masonry is the attainment of Light, and its first principle is Brotherly Love, it is not to be wondered at that these two great figures became its patron Saints one the leader of those who are seeking the Light, the other the teacher of those who have found it. For the same reason they are honored on the festal days of the old, beautiful Light religion of humanity St. John the Baptist amid the splendor of summer, St. John the Divine at the winter solstice when the mighty orb of Light is most remote from us.

John the Baptist was a prophet, "a son of the Voice of God," in the old Hebrew phrase; "yea, and more than a prophet," said the Teacher whose advent he foretold. "There hath not arisen among them that are born of women a greater than John the Baptist." No man ever won higher eulogy; no one ever more richly deserved it. What is prophecy? It is two things-forth-telling and fore-telling. The prophets have been for the most part forth-tellers, the great burden of their messages being the exposition and application of moral truths. Yet ever and again they have seen the clouds clear from the sky of the future, and have caught glimpses of a light upon the far-away hills of Time. They have seen, as men see in dreams, places, cities, august figures, vast upheavals impending, and felt the incommunicable thrill of advancing destinies. It is therefore that they speak in words cryptic and vague, foreshadowing in dim and awful form the fashion of things to be.

Such was St. John the Baptist; a rebuker of kings, a scorner of sham, a denouncer of iniquity, whose speech was swift, startling, eruptive, turgid, tearing away every thin veil of pretense and bringing men face to face with eternal realities. Austere, aloof, uncompromising, he saw clearly, felt deeply, spoke plainly; and if he lacked those great fertilizing ideas out which new religions grow, he had a vast capacity for moral indignation. Mere formalism evoked his withering satire. Profession without performance provoked his blistering scorn. Hypocrisy he flayed with whips of fire. Terrible in speech, he was yet tender of heart, and when the storm of his eloquence has passed by the qualities that stand out in his life are his exalted purity of soul, his passion for righteousness, his courage, his sincerity, his self-effacing humility, his grand magnanimity, his rugged nobility of character and his heroism in death.

Truly, Masonry makes profession of high ideals when it invokes John the Baptist as its patron Saint! Were he to appear at one of our festivals on his day, what would be his message to the men of today who dedicate their Lodges in his honor? Would his old indignation flash out upon us, rebuking us for our snug contentment, our smug self-satisfaction, our worship of the past, and our ritualism without reality? Would he not say to us today, as he did to the men of old, that we must repent in our hearts and show by our deeds the sincerity of our professions and the sanctity of our vows made at the altar of righteousness? These are things to think about on St. John's Day, and if we are worthy to meet in his name they will make us pause and ponder, the while we search our hearts.

Has Masonry, so eager to honor a great Prophet, no prophetic element in it today? Has it no vision, no dream, no forward-looking program, no creative purpose for the times to be? Has its altar light faded into the poor flicker of a painted fire? Or will it become an inspired teacher of righteousness as the sovereign reality of the universe, the solitary hope of humanity and the secure foundation of personal and social life! Will it put a new dignity into its degrees, a new fire into its philosophy, and tell the young men who throng its temple gates that they must prove their faith by their deeds, and keep their vows in the home, in the marts of trade, in the state, and thus foretell the coming of a nobler social order, a juster state, and a more humane civilization! Size does not signify. Numbers do not count. But righteous manhood is everything!

THE MEASURE OF A MAN

Masonry, being an exact science, and coming to us adown the ages from a time when mathematics had mystical meanings, has much to say about numbers and measurement. The numbers Three, Five and Seven, that so frequently occur in our ritual, had for the Oriental mind an eloquence which we do not fully appreciate. Hints of this meet us in our New Testament, especially in the strange and solemn visions of the Apocalypse. In that book, Three is the signature of Deity. Four indicates the world of created things. Seven denotes peace and covenant, while Ten is the symbol of completeness. In the ancient days, numbers indicated words, suggested thoughts, revealed truths. As Ruskin studied the Basilica of St. Mark, finding in each column or statue a history and a lesson, so we may study the ancient structure of Masonry.

What did Plato mean when he said that God is the great Geometrician, and that by the art of measurement, the soul of man is saved? Wherefore should Masonry make use of number and measure, if it be not to show us the Measure of a Man, since what we think of God, of life, of the world, comes back at last and always to what we think of Man. The old Greek thinkers saw this in an early time, and set it forth in their incisive and vivid manner. "Man is the measure of all things," said Protagoras. "No, said Plato, "God, the Divine Mind, is the measure of all things." Then came Aristotle, one of the noblest thinkers whose genius ever glorified humanity, and with his profounder insight united the two, when he said: "It is the perfect man, in whom the thought of God is clear, who is the measure of all things." Here again it is a matter of Measurement, and in that fine art lies the secret of knowledge and of life.

No doubt this was what the Seer on Patmos meant by his vivid and detailed description of the Holy City, as though he would have us know that it is no phantom city but a reality. So real is it that his guide carries a reed with which to measure the city, and register how high its towers rise in the units of human reckoning, Then he pauses, as if someone had asked him how our earthly cubits can form a calculus for that which is outside of Time; and he adds a parenthesis to resolve the doubt, "according to the measure of a man, that is, of the angel." Man is a citizen of two worlds, but he has no skill to realize the Unseen world save by the aid of the world of sense. As often as he tries to ponder, in reverence, what is the nature of the Supreme Architect, he finds himself thinking of Him by the help of those moral qualities which he sees, dimly enough, in the best men he has known. If he asks, wistfully, about the life to come, the only answer is one expressed in the ideas and images, the forms and colors, of the life that now is.

He cannot help himself; there is no other way for him to think. Unless truth, justice, goodness in man be the same as truth, justice and goodness in God, then we know not anything, nor can we ever learn; and we ought in honesty to enclose the word God in quotation marks. They are the same, in quality at least, however much they may differ in degree; and this is the basis of all our higher human life. Our age-long tragedy is that our race has measured its life by the animal rather than the angel calculus. Masonry asks us to measure up to our highest, that is, to the Angel within us, with which agree all the sages who, as Dante says, teach us "how man can make his life eternal." Long ago Ovid said, "It is the mind that makes the man, and our measure is in our immortal souls." And Plato laid down the principle of true living when he wrote: "The right way is to place the goods of the soul first in the scale, and in the second place, the goods of the body, and in the third place, those of money and property." Any other order is an inversion of values, and ends in tragedy.

Well, may the ancient singer pray that we may so number our days, that we may attain to this true wisdom, if so that the beauty of the eternal may be upon us, and the work of our hands be established. When shall we become that which we are? cried Maeterlink. Such is the Doctrine of the Measure, so eloquently taught by Masonry, and he is wise, who has ears to hear and a heart to heed.

"Held our eyes no sunny sheen,

How could God's own light be seen?

Dwelt no power divine within us,

How could God's divineness win us

THE DOCTRINE OF THE BALANCE

READERS of Albert Pike will recall the stately pages with which Morals and Dogma closes, setting forth, in a manner unforgettable, the Doctrine of the Balance. Many had taught this truth before time out of mind, no one more impressively than the man whom Pike was richly indebted, but his exposition is none the less his own. With vast labor he brings together his findings, showing that to this result the wisdom of the ages runs, what the sages have thought equally with what the mystics have dreamed. Always it is a triad, suggested by the ancient idea of the number Three, the singular, the dual and the plural, the odd and even added, and the great emblem of the Triangle, symbol of perfection. It is seen in all Masonic symbolism, from end to end and at every step of the Mystic quest for the secret which every Mason is seeking.

Eloquently, and with every variation of emphasis and illustration, he lays the matter before us, carrying it into all the fields of human activity and aspiration. Sympathy and Antipathy, Attraction and Repulsion, Fate and Freedom, each a fact of life and a force of nature, are contraries alike in the universe and in the soul of man, wherein we see eternity in miniature. As the earth is held in its orbit by the action of opposing forces, so truth is made up of two opposite propositions, as peace lies in the union of motion and rest, and harmony is the fruit of seeming war. Here he finds the solution of the problem of the One and the Many, of the Infinite and the Finite, of Unity amidst Manifoldness: the principle of the Balance, the secret of the universal equilibrium:

"Of that Equilibrium in the Deity, between the Infinite Divine Wisdom and the Infinite Divine Power; from which result the Stability of the Universe, the unchangeableness of the Divine Law, and the Principles of Truth, Justice, and Right which are a part of it; . . . Of that Equilibrium also, between the Infinite Divine Justice and the Infinite Divine Mercy, the result of which is the Infinite Divine Equity, and the Moral Harmony or Beauty of the Universe. By it the endurance of created and imperfect natures in the presence of a Perfect Deity is made possible; . . .

Of that Equilibrium between Necessity and Liberty, between the action of the Divine Omnipotence and the Free-will of man, by which vices and base actions, and ungenerous thoughts and words are crimes and wrongs, justly punished by the law of cause and consequence, though nothing in the universe can happen or be done contrary to the will of God; and without which co-existence of Liberty and Necessity, of Free-will in the creature and Omnipotence in the Creator, there could be no religion, nor any law of right and wrong, or merit or demerit, nor any justice in human punishments or penal laws.

And, finally, of that Equilibrium, possible in ourselves, and which Masonry incessantly labors to accomplish in its Initiates, and demands of its Adepts and Princes else unworthy of their titles between the Spiritual and Divine and the Material and human in man; between the Intellect, Reason, and Moral Sense on one side, and the Appetites and Passions on the other, from which result the Harmony and Beauty of a well-regulated life." And so on, through a passage of singular elevation both of language and of thought, we are led by an ancient truth which becomes a vision in the mind of a nobler thinker. My design is not to add to his exposition, but to apply it with emphasis and illustration, if so that it may be brought home to our "business and bosom" and be of real service to us in the life which we live together, and in the life which each must live alone. For it is the high service of Masonry that it puts a man in the straight path which the wisest of the race have walked, leading him midway between the falsehood of extremes, and bringing the highest teaching of the past to the uses of the present. After all, how to live is the one matter; and he is wise who joins the goodly Shakespeare gospel of Courage, Sanity and Pity with that other Gospel of Faith, Hope, and Love. Every man will need all the aid he can get, unless he be content, as no real man can be, to live in the world as a mere looker-on at a drama in which others are actors,

"In God's vast house a curious guest, Seeing how all works take their flight."

From bottom to top, life is a contradiction and a paradox, and the beginning of wisdom is to know that fact and adjust ourselves to it. Light and darkness, heat and cold, mind and matter, fate and free-will, asceticism and indulgence, socialism and anarchy, dogmatism and doubt, reason and authority, no man may ever hope to live long enough, much less to think deeply enough, to harmonize these paradoxes. The way of wisdom is to accept both facts in each case, as the Two Pillars of a Temple of Truth, and walk between them into the hush of the holy place. Either one, without the other, is only a half-truth which ends in perversion, if not in insanity, turning the hearty, wholesome, clear seeing spirit of manhood into the pitiful narrowness and hardness of a bigot or a fanatic.

For example: "All is free, that is false: all is fate, that is false. All things are free and fated, that is true." It is possible to make an argument in behalf of fatalism so freezing that one is left with the feeling that he is no more responsible for his thoughts and acts, than he is for the shape of his head and the color of his eyes. Having listened to such an argument, each of us may say, as Dr. Johnson did, "I know I am free, and that's the end on it." On the other side, one can present a thesis in proof of the freedom of man so convincing that fate seems a fiction. Both are true, and the great truth consists of two opposites which are not contradictory that it is the Fate of man to be Free if he fights for it, approves himself worthy of it, uniting his will with the Will of the Master of the World! Otherwise, we men are slaves journeying downward "to the dust of graves," slaves of greed and passion and a fatal folly.

Asceticism is one extreme, indulgence, another. One would repress every natural instinct in behalf of a pale, wan purity; the other would follow every fancy, driven hither and yon by every gust of passion, at the mercy of every caprice. Between the two lies temperance, keeping the balance between two absurdities, making a right use of everything, and abusing nothing; its motto the wise words of the old Greeks, "In nothing too much." Socialism seems to hold that the State is everything, the Individual nothing, or at best only a cog in a vast machine, an atom in an indistinguishable blur. Anarchy makes the State nothing, and the Individual everything, each a law unto himself, and chaos at the end. Between the two lies the way of wise government in which "Freedom slowly broadens down from precedent to precedent," or grows gladly up from the life of a just and intelligent people. There are certain things which every man must surrender in behalf of the common good, and other things which it were a sin to abdicate, the while a shifting, zig-zag line runs between dividing the man from the mass.

By the same token, in religion Dogmatism affirms everything, makes a map of the Infinite, and an atlas of Eternity, so certain is it of things whereof no man knoweth. It talks of God as if He were a man in the next room. It knows the origin of all things, and the final destiny of humanity. Doubt denies everything, questions the competence of the human mind to know Divine things, leaving us with the assurance that nothing is certain but uncertainty; nothing secure but insecurity. Again, it is the doctrine of the balance, as in the natural world peace is found amid the poise of powers. Between dogmatism and doubt is a wise and reverent Faith, which dares to say, "Now we know in part, a tiny part, no doubt, but knowledge is real as far as it goes, and what we know gives us confidence in the vast Unknown. And so, we make bold to trust the ultimate decency of things and the veiled kindness of the Father of men, assured that He who has brought us to where we are will lead us to where we ought to be!"

Of this fundamental paradox of life, the Cross is the symbol. Older than Christianity, as old, almost, as human life, it is the supreme symbol of the race. When man first emerged from the "old dark backward and abysm of time," he had a cross in his hand. Where he got it, what he meant by it, many may conjecture but no one knows. The Cross, like life itself, is also a collision and a contradiction, its four arms pointing every whither, making it the great guide-post of free thought. As long as a man keeps his poise, never forgetting the profound paradox at the heart of all high thought, he may think as far and as fast as his mind can go. For many of us, of course, the Cross is hallowed anew and forever by the name of One whose life was a tragedy, whose love was heroic in its gentleness, who wins by "that strange power called weakness," whose character is the sovereign wonder of the world, and whose spirit is the holiest tradition of humanity.

Since this is so, since the way of sanity, if not of salvation, lies in keeping our balance, why is it that men lose their poise? No man of us, when he thinks of the days agone, but recalls acts which he not only regrets, but which puzzle him by their strange stupidity. He would give almost as much to be able to understand them as he would to forget them. Why is this so? Shakespeare has much to teach us here, much of abiding profit to remember, if so that we may understand the past and make a better use of the future. He everywhere shows that tragedy is the fruit of treachery, and that treachery has its roots in obsession, someone thing that gets so close to the mind that it can see nothing else, blinds it, preys upon it, making a man first a fanatic, and then, it may be, a criminal. Macbeth was a man of noble nature; his wife was a lovely lady. They became obsessed with ambition for place and power, and to what dark depths of sin and shame that mad blindness led them that terrible tragedy tells us. This lesson, taught so often by our supreme poet, is for each of us, teaching us to keep our poise, and to flee an obsession as a plague. Whatever fastens itself upon the mind, shutting out the light, marring the proportions and perspectives of things, forebodes disaster.

Perhaps it is physical passion. If so, it will turn love into lust and make the world a bawdy-house. It may be political ambition, and a man throws everything to the winds in order to win, forgetting that no office on earth is worth the sacrifice of integrity, and, also, if he wins by trickery he is unfit to hold it. It may be religion. Think of the crimes unspeakable, the brutalities unbelievable, which have been committed by men in a frenzy of fanatical bigotry-dipping their hands in blood and thinking they were doing the will of God! They were madmen. Plato said that all men are more or less insane, and that the man whom we put in a straight-jacket is only a little more emphatically out of his mind than the rest of us. The more reason, then, why we should keep our poise and walk the quiet way of sanity and charity, in love of God and man.

After this manner we expound the Doctrine of the Balance, as taught by Pike, reminding our Brethren, as we remind ourselves, that the wisdom of life lies in freedom, serenity, and forgiveness, in victory by self-surrender to the highest laws of life, and that we dare not turn either to the right or the left. By such teaching, men become happy and free; in this way, we may grow old without being sad, and wise without being cynical; and learn, at last, that everlasting gentleness which is the highest wisdom man may win from the hard facts and the often strange medley of his days. Let us also lay to heart the prayer quoted by Pike:

"Let Him, the ever-living God, be always present in thy mind; for thy mind itself is His likeness, for it, too, is invisible and impalpable, and without form. As He exists forever, so thou also, when thou shalt put off this which is visible and corruptible, shalt stand before Him forever, living and endowed with knowledge."

TRAVEL SKETCHS

ON THE SEA

Prompt to the minute, on June 17, at noon, the Philadelphia moved from her pier and slowly turned to the open sea. The orchestra was playing, the decks were crowded, and perhaps a thousand people were waving farewells among them, a good Brother Mason who was kind enough to come and bid me goodbye. It was a scene not soon to be forgotten. Surely, there is something infinite in every parting, and never more so than when the Sea is to separate us. Soon individual faces faded, and we could only see the handkerchiefs fluttering signals of goodwill-handkerchiefs wet with tears.

New York, seen from the harbor, is a great picture indeed, albeit made less vivid by a haze of smoke and fog that hung over it. Suddenly the sun broke through the mist, and it seemed like a fairy city seen in a dream, a land of fairy cliff-dwellers! No wonder Poole wrote his story of The Harbor and the romance of it. But the picture does not remain long, save in memory where our pictures hang. Dimmer and dimmer it grows, until at last it is a blur, and then a thin blue line, and finally it fades. No one may put into words his feelings at such an hour, when for the first time he leaves his native land and turns to the great open sea!

And the Sea! For an inlander like myself, it is a thing of wonder, at once a fact and a figure, a symbol and a parable. Like sky, like sea. If the sky is gray, so is the sea. If blue, the sea is blue, such a dark, rich blue. But it was very gray when we set sail. Soon a fog fell over us and we could hardly see the boat that met us to take our pilot off. And that fog-horn is terrifying! What would life be if all our dangers made that much noise. Perhaps they do, only we do not hear the warnings.

But the fog soon lifted, like a curtain, and revealed the Sea, The Sea! the Sea! so wide and grand, stretching away into infinity-yea, "The Sea is His, and He made it." All day long the great words of the Bible about the Sea kept coming to mind, with new meanings I had never guessed before. Truly, that old Book is like a harp which says for us what our poor, dumb words cannot say. "There is sorrow upon the sea; it cannot be still," what words they are as one looks out over those restless, reinless waters. And there came also those other words, so freighted with meaning just now, "and the sea gave up the dead that were in it." But best of all, the line of the Psalmist, "Thy way, O Lord, is in the sea."

Really, if I were a rich Pagan instead of a poor Mason, I would build a temple to the Sea. It is so strong and deep, so patient, merciful, and gracious, to ship or soul that bravely casts loose upon its mighty promises; so variable and cruel to the unpiloted and unseaworthy. It is a great burden-bearer. It cannot be overloaded. It cannot be broken down. It never grows weary. It never needs repairs. Also, it is a great physician. It rests the eye with its overpowering vastness of outlook. It calms the heart with its greatness and its never-ending music. It speaks to the mind of that Divine abyss over which the mystics brood but never fathom. It responds to every mood, now sad, now glad, now quietly meditative; it answers every call of the imagination, and can preach more sermons than all preachers. Besides, it is a great teacher. It lays its mighty law upon the restless spirit and tells us to stop sputtering, be still, listen, and know. And as we listen, the sighs of human care are lost in the murmur of its many waters. At last Restlessness, cut off from its supplies, surrenders to Rest.

Why did St. John leave the Sea out of his vision of heaven? He foresaw a time when "there shall be no more sea." Why so? No doubt the exile on the Isle of Patmos, longing for the fair city of Ephesus, the scene of his ministry, and hungering for the sight of familiar faces, grew weary of the imprisoning sea. Sundered by leagues of tumbling waves from those he loved, he dreamed of a world where there would be "no sea." But it is not so now, not so much so at least. Once the symbol of separation, the sea has become a bond of union between lands and peoples. Once the dread of daring sailors, who, despite their dread, braved its dangers and discovered its paths, it has become the servant of man, yielding to the quiet power of intelligence. The sea of which Homer and Virgil sing is the unknown, untamed sea. We today sail a sea whose ways, waves and winds are an open book, and whose forces have been converted into beneficent ministries.

Still, Matthew Arnold speaks of "unplumbed, salt, estranging sea," by which he meant the awful isolation of each soul in an unfathomable universe. More often in English poetry, and indeed in all poetry, since Homer, that has in it the sound of the sea, the tidal rhythms of the sea, its measured waves and its immeasurable horizons, have been the great symbols of the Divine depth and mystery; just as the stars round off the three divisions of the Divine Comedy of Dante. The music of this deeper and more eternal sea rolls through all great poetry, and nowhere with more melody than in Shakespeare, who caught the very cadence of that unfathomable sea whose waves are years and whose depth is eternity.

How can a man be irreligious on the Sea? Are we not, all of us, now and forever, out on the bosom of the deep, with the infinite above, beneath, and about us? We feel secure enough indeed, thanks largely to the cheerful company, the dear faces, the duties and pieties of the day.

Still, when at times we look over the edge of the boat, up starts a primitive terror which only faith can allay. Religion is a thing of the depths and for the depths. "Have mercy upon me, O Lord, my boat is so small, and Thine ocean is so great," in that cry of the old Breton fisherman we have the profound instinct which lies at the heart of faith. Reason may serve us in shallow waters, but when life takes us beyond our depth, as it so often does, faith saves us. There will be companies of believing souls, so long as there are deep, unplumbed places in this life of ours.

But here I am preaching, as usual, from force of habit, no doubt. Yet there are worse things one could be guilty of. Moreover, I cannot help it. Last night I sat up on the upper deck of the ship near the prow, at midnight, long after others had gone to bed, except, of course, the guzzlers in the saloon. It was a clear cool night of stars, and the great sea lay spread out beneath. It was a still and holy hour in which the sea and the stars told me many things. Never did the great old words, "What is man, that Thou art mindful of him?" come home with such awful majesty of simple truth to subdue the heart and still it. And yet, never did I have a more vivid sense of the greatness and worth of the soul as in that solemn trysting time. Then the ship bell rang out the hour, the watchman above cried, "All's Well," and I went to my couch knowing that if I sank it would be not into the sea, but beyond it!

Thus and so our good ship of Brotherly Love sails on and on, out over the blue rim of the world. Again and again, one turns away from the Human Comedy on board to the mighty Sea whose lonely waters drift and sing! How indifferent it is to our human doings and undoings, how deaf to our jabbering gossip, its white caps suggesting shining teeth showing in laughter at our vanities. It knows nothing of the greatness of Kitchener, and buries him as quickly as it does the poor stoker dropped into a vast and wandering grave. Merciful when we obey her, merciless when we disobey, she lulls us to sleep at night as if the ship were a cradle rocked by an unseen hand. I have fallen in love with the Sea. As long as I live, its mighty waters will whisper to my heart of "that immortal sea which brought us hither," and will receive us to its bosom "when that which drew from out the boundless deep, turns again home." Whatever betide, it is enough to know that,

"There is a wideness in God's mercy,
Like the wideness of the Sea."

At Sea, June 22.

MARQUIS DE LAFAYETTE

MUCH was said during the early days of the world-war now raging as to the attitude of our Republic in the crisis; and opinions differed regarding our debt to France as compared with that to Germany, for aid given during our War of the Revolution. Both of those countries sent assistance of various kinds. Whatever the degree of obligation, it is the simple fact that of all the men who came over to aid the colonists in their struggle, the name of Lafayette has come down to us with a peculiar luster. Questions have been raised as to the motives, high or low, disinterested or selfish, which led these men into the war. Bearing upon this question, in respect of Lafayette, it is interesting to read what is said about him in "The Household of the Lafayette's," by Edith Sichel, as follows:

"One night, in 1776, the Marshal de Broglie was giving a dinner party in honor of the Duke of Gloucester. This light-hearted brother of George III regaled the company with accounts of the American revolt, and especially of the affair of the tea in Boston Harbor. His sympathy was with the rebels, and he dwelt on their need of recruits. The guests were men of high rank, and gorgeous uniforms were much in evidence. Almost unnoticed among them sat a young man of nineteen, silent, solemn, absorbed in listening; he was thin, red-haired, hook-nosed, and awkward. After the dinner was over, he strode across the hall to the Duke of Gloucester, outwardly calm, but repressing deep emotion. "I will join those Americans," he cried. "I will help them fight for freedom. Tell me how to set about it." He was the Marquis de Lafayette, not long married; and it has been said of him that his whole life was ruled by two passions-love for his wife, and love of freedom."

Ninety-two years ago, New York City witnessed the most enthusiastic celebration of the birthday of Lafayette in the history of our Republic. Lafayette himself was present, on his final and memorable visit to the country whose struggle for independence he so nobly aided. Instead of thirteen weak colonies, he found twenty-four prosperous States. His journey through the States was an ovation of patriotic gratitude and pride, and he returned ladened with all the honors which a nation can bestow. On May 20th, 1834, he died in Paris in his seventy-seventh year, gracious gentleman, a knightly soldier, an honored and beloved member of the Masonic fraternity.

TRAVEL SKETCHES

LONDON TOWN

YES, it is London. Had I been set down here from anywhere, or from nowhere, I should have known that it was old London town. Here all things turn to the left, as they do in the Inferno of Dante, there is no mistaking the place. And speaking of the Inferno, the English way of handling baggage gives one a clear idea of what that place must be like.

How quiet London is. Compared with the din of New York and the hideous nightmare of the Chicago loop, it is as quiet as a country village. There are no sky-scrapers to be seen, but the scene spread out like a panorama from the top of Primrose Hill is not to be forgotten! Yes, it is London, the greatest city in the world, and not another like it. But which London is it? Well, that depends upon what London you are looking for.

There are many London's, my dear reader. There is the London of the Tower and the Abbey, of SoHo and the Strand, of Buckingham and Downing Street, to say nothing of Piccadilly. There is the London of the story-book; of Whittington and his Cat and Goody Two-Shoes and the Canterbury Shades; of Shakespeare and Marlowe and Chatterton; of Nell Gwynne and Dick Steele and poor old Noll-aye, the London of all that is bizarre in history or strange in romance.

They are all here, with much else in this gigantic medley of past and present, of misery and magnificence. Sometimes for me it is hard to know which holds closest, the London of Fiction or the London of History, or that London which is a mingling of both the London of Literature. Anyway, as I see it, Goldsmith carouses with

Tom Jones, and Harry Fielding discusses philosophy with the Vicar of Wakefield; Nicholas Nickleby makes bold to introduce himself to Mr. W. H. Thackeray and to ask his favor in behalf of a poor artist, the son of a hair-dresser in Maiden Lane; and Boz, as he passes through Fleet Street, is tripped by an Artful Dodger and falls into the arms of St. Charles Lamb.

No doubt my London is in large part a dream, not to say a fool's paradise, but it is most enchanting. Slowly it works its ancient spell, and he who does not love it is fit for strategems and spoils, not fit for anything, I had almost said. There is no denying, I am in love with London, and can drink as much tea as any Englishman who ever coveted his neighbors goods. Here is the center of the world, so far as I am concerned, the great old city of the motherland of all my fathers-everywhere the hauntings of history, a scene to stir the soul of one who loves England equally for its fiction and its fact.

Yesterday I visited the Abbey and attended the afternoon service, an hour I can never live long enough to forget. How can I express my feeling as I stood for the first time in that grey old pile thinking of the mighty dead who sleep there, thinking how those pillars have stood through all the nights and days, through storm and calm, peace and war, for ages. Truly, "time, the white god, makes all things holy, and what is old becomes religion." I sat facing the Poet's Corner, where Tennyson and Browning sleep side by side, as they should in the eternal fitness of things, and the effigy of Shakespeare has the bust of Burns nearby. If one cannot pray in Westminster Abbey, where men have prayed for centuries, and where the echo of voices long hushed still cling to its arches, he cannot pray at all, unless it be on the wide and eloquent sea!

Today I went to St. Paul's and heard the Archbishop of Canterbury preach, and after the service, wandered for two hours in the recesses of the cathedral. Descending into the crypt, one looks upon the tomb of Nelson, the mighty lord of the sea, and the sleeping place of Wellington, the great commander of the English race. Lord Roberts rests a few feet away. Here sleep the great artists, as the poets are honored in the Abbey, among them Wren who built St. Paul's, a famous Mason. Who can measure the influence of such a building, enshrining as it does so many historic memories, the dust of great men, and the tradition of ages of patriotism and prayer? It stands for order in the streets, for order in the land, for order in the secret places of the soul!

From St. Paul's it is not a far walk across London Bridge to Southwark Cathedral, hardly less interesting and far less known. In this parish stood the Globe theatre, in which Shakespeare made himself and England famous, and there is a recumbent figure of the poet in alabaster, the gift of Americans. His younger brother lies buried there in company with Massinger and Fletcher. Indeed, it had been a place of literary renown long before Shakespeare, in the days of Gower, who rests there, and Chaucer, whose Canterbury pilgrims set out from the Tabard Inn, once close at hand. Also, in this parish was born John Harvard, founder of our great university, and there is a chapel in his honor in the cathedral. And so my story might go on endlessly.

Old London is the keeper of a great history, but the London of today is athrill and athrob with the stir of history in the making. How impressive to step out of some grey old church, like that of St. Bartholomew, or the Temple where poor Noll found rest at last, into the teeming, tragic London of today; from the peace of the past into the tense air of the greatest war in all the annals of time. If the London of old is hallowing, London of today is thrilling, sometimes terrifying. There is a sense of a vast tragedy only a few miles away, and here one is behind the scenes, so to speak, soldiers and sailors everywhere;

armies of nurses, Red Cross emblems, ambulances, hospitals, and so forth.

How striking the contrast as one steps out of the quiet of the past where "the eternal ages watch and wait." Indeed, just now England is a world of women nurses, messengers, porters, tram and bus conductors, very conscious and important in uniform and badge and brass buttons. Manifestly the English woman is finding herself and she likes it. Bright-eyed, capable, and cheerful, she is doing things she never dreamed of doing before. Even women doing their ancient work as house-wives feel a new distinction, I dare say, and dust their rooms for the good of the country. They have learned their worth to the nation in a new way. Will they be willing to go back to the old ways after war? Can they do it? What will be the result? Will not England be permanently different?

Such questions have followed me ever since I landed. At Hyde Park entrance the other day I saw one of the shrieking sisterhood which I thought were extinct, I wish they were. Maybe I shall live long enough to forget that sight, but I doubt it. Hideous is a mild word. Fact is, my profession will not allow me to say what I really feel. Those poor, half-crazed creatures have set their cause back fifty years in England, and injured it everywhere. Had I been shaky on the subject of suffrage, that harangue, and still more the wild-eyed fanaticism of the ranter, would have sent me away with a vast disgust. Heaven help a cause that has such advocates.

But she and the like of her are forgotten when one sees the heroic spirit of the multitudes of women who work and endure, counting their sorrow as only one item in a measureless common woe. And they are so brave and gay withal. Indeed, London is unnaturally gay and many are puzzled by it, knowing not what it means. Almost every reporter who has interviewed me, and they have been legion, has brought up the subject. Yet it ought to be very easy to understand. A man who had been in the trenches told me that there men learn to live a moment at a time, they may not be alive more than a moment. And the reaction, he said, an explosion of "insane gaiety," to use his words. Pent up feelings must find vent, and it is no wonder that the theatres are crowded every night, and the more rollicking the play the greater the jam.

Frankly, I was not prepared for the feeling against America which exists in England today, and I am amazed at it. It is widespread, and is sometimes so intense as to verge on anti-Americanism. My English friends assure me that it is not so in a way that really matters, but I know better, and Americans living here confirm my impression. Perhaps it is not so with those who are discerning, but with the man-in-street it is different. He feels, however wrongly, that America betrayed humanity in behalf of dollars. It is not so much that the president kept us out of the war, but the appalling way in which he did it, that hurts.

Further, the American government is a continuing entity to English people. They do not divide it into presidential terms or personalities, and the feeling against America will continue whatever the future may be in our politics. Therefore, it behooves us to do all within our power, on both sides of the sea, to see that such a feeling does not gather force and grow; for, surely, the last and worst calamity that could befall humanity would be an estrangement between the Empire and the Republic having one language, one tradition, and one common ideal of civilization. But I am off my subject and had better go back to London.

The newspapers here interest me very much. They are small now, to be sure, except Old Thunderer, the Times, owing to the price of paper and the lack of labor. They are poorly printed, as compared with our papers, certainly the religious papers are abominably printed. But they are better written by far. They serve the news up after their fashion in more compact form, but in a much more lucid style, and some of the war correspondents, Phillips Gibbs more than any other, methinks, are very remarkable. Also, the editorial page has more influence than with us, though it has suffered decline, I am told, on this side. Men of letters write more frequently for the daily press than with us. Certainly the press, both in London and in the provinces, has been very kind to me in every way.

I am bound to say that religious conditions in England are most distressing and confounding. The churches are empty, for the most part, and have little influence, the state church emptier than the rest, if possible. Perhaps I should have said church conditions instead, for some of my thoughtful friends tell me that there is more religion outside of the church than inside. Carlyle thought it was so in his day. Anyway, I have attended three religious conferences since I came, representing three branches of the church, and the tone of bewilderment and discouragement was common to all. They know not what to do, and the ministers are all the time trying to explain the war and "to justify the ways of God to man" with not much success, I must admit. It makes me think of a student in the University of Michigan, after three visiting ministers had each discussed the question of the existence of God. He said that up until that time he had never had any doubts, but that now he was a little uncertain. I am much in his case, as to the explanations I have heard so far.

There is a vast unbridged, and seemingly unbridgeable-gulf between the church and what is called the working classes; and it widens every day. What the end will be is hard to know. If the war did not save dear old England from something like revolution, it at least postponed it. Perhaps the shaking the war has given the churches will wake them up, before it is too late. For surely the people are as religious as ever they were, but the churches no longer express their religion. There are exceptions, of course, to all these statements, thank heaven, but I am speaking of the general condition.

And the City Temple is an exception to anything on earth. It is wonderful, all that I expected and more. It has been full from top to bottom at every service a sea of faces below and clouds of faces in the galleries. What a sight! What an opportunity! What a crushing responsibility! If anybody ever tells me that an English audience is unresponsive, I shall be ready to fight him. It is not so. I never had such a response, much less such a welcome, in any strange place in all my life. And if anything had been lacking at the Temple, it would have been made up by the Masons at their brilliant banquet and reception in my honor. That, too, was a scene never to be forgotten till all things fade in the dark. Of this more anon.

THE LAMP OF FELLOWSHIP

RUSKIN lighted his Seven Lamps of Architecture and set them on golden candlesticks, the better to show us that the laws of art are moral laws, whether they are used in building a cathedral or in making a character. If we would build for eternity, he tells us that we must obey Him whose mountain peaks and forest aisles we imitate in our temples. Martineau lighted five Watch-night Lamps, in a noble address, and urged us to keep our souls awake looking for the dawn in "this solemn eve of an eternal day which we call Human Life."

But there is another Lamp without which all lights flicker and fade as we walk together in the dim country of this world, the Lamp of Fellowship. Indeed, one may sum up the whole of life, and of religion, in the one-word Fellowship, a deep and tender fellowship of the soul with the Father of all, whose inspiration and help are the supreme facts of life; and then, turning manward, to fill all the relations of life with the spirit of sincere and sympathetic fellowship. What more than this can the best man do; how better can he serve his fellow pilgrims who journey with him the old-worn human way?

> "Fellowship is heaven,
> Lack of fellowship is hell."

By the same token, if the soul of Masonry is its Symbolism, its heart-throb is felt in its Spirit of Fellowship. Its history is gray with age. Its philosophy is profound. Its philanthropies are beautiful and benign. Its ritual is rich in suggestion, eloquent with echoes of those truths that have haunted the mind of man since thought found a throne in the brain. But the heart of Masonry, its vital force, its divine fire are in its Strong Grip by which men of every land, of every creed, of every shade of temperament and thought are brought together on the five points of Fellowship!

Fellowship, that is the word which utters, so far as any word may utter, the deepest reality and the highest aspiration in the heart of Masonry. This is the mystery which its rituals labor to express and which its symbols seek to interpret and unfold a mystery, as Whitman said, more profound than metaphysics, by which man is united with his Fellows in Faith, Freedom, and Friendship. For this Masonry exists, to assert the fact, to spread the spirit, and to promote the practice of Brotherhood, that man may learn that it is what he shares that makes life worth living, and that "he who seeks his own loses the things in common."

Indeed, the whole arrangement of human life exists that man may learn three things: the law of right, love of God, and love of man. After long ages of tragedy we are beginning to learn the first lesson, that a world in which poison makes men strong and food destroys them is not more unreal than a world in which falsehood makes great characters and righteousness issues in ignoble spirit and unworthy life. How far we have failed to learn the other two truths of love of God and love of man, the human scene makes pitifully plain. Yet learn them we must, else the story of men will be blurred with blood and blistered with tears till whatever is to be the end of things, with never any hope of a better day to be.

Here lies the divine mission of Masonry, to fulfill which we must make deep research into our history, and still more into our hearts, using every art at our command, every influence we can invoke, joining our hands in one high service, the while we light the Lamp of Fellowship and learn to "live in the eternal order which never dies."

This is the work on the Trestle-board for Brethren everywhere,

For never was there greater need for level, plumb, and square,

For trowel with cement of love to strengthen and unite

The human race in Brotherhood, and usher in the Light!

TRAVEL SKETCHES

STRATFORD ON AVON

WHAT a day was that on which I went to Stratford, to visit a tiny town and a mighty grave! It was like a dream come true, its soft bright hours like the stanzas of a poem in which echoes of unheard music linger. All the way down from London I mused on the mystery of genius, but found no key to the riddle of it. God breathes it; beyond that we cannot go. Dig how you will in the lore of Stratford, no fact, no hint turns up to account for a man whose genius is "an intellectual ocean whose waves touch every shore." It is a mystery the secret of which no one may fathom.

My guide, philosopher and friend took pains that I should see everything, and to best advantage. Climbing into a cab, we turned away from the town out into the country. It was like riding through a park. Hedgerows neatly trimmed, a quaint cottage here and there, apricots on garden walls, birds singing, and over all the dreamy peace of English summer! Where we were going I did not know. Nor did I much care, wishing that the ride might be endless amid scenes so lovely, thinking of a boy who once wandered along these ways. After a little we turned a corner and stopped at a long, low cottage with a thatched roof and tiny windows, and flowers in the garden.

Then I knew where we were and why we had come. It was the home of Ann Hathaway, where the boy had gone a courting in the village of Shottery. Near the front door is a stone where Dickens once sat musing of that odd romance of long ago, remembering, no doubt, how the boy himself had afterwards said that it would be a good thing if every boy could be put soundly to sleep at fifteen, and not be allowed to wake up until he is twenty-three. Of a truth it would be safer, but think of the fun he would miss! Inside the cottage they show you the old kitchen, with its old fireplace but little changed since Will and Ann sat so close together on the seat nearby, whispering all the sweet nothings that lads and lassies say when life is new and love is young.

Thence we drove to Borden's Hill, a mile or more away, from which lay spread out, as in a picture, the town of Stratford, its rows of brick houses, its winding streets, its church-spire, half hidden by trees. It is a scene to haunt the heart forever, and 'tis no wonder that memories of it floated into all the plays and poems of the Bard of Avon. Nor is it strange that Shakespeare came back to this scene towards the end, wise enough to know when to quit and wishing to leave the earth where he had first learned to love it. Down the Hill we went, our next stop being at the house on Henley Street, where the seer was born. Forty thousand people visit that house every year, coming from the ends of the earth to pay homage to a great memory.

No one knows in what room the poet was born, but tradition has consecrated the small chamber facing the street, on the first floor. Names have been scribbled over all the walls. Most of them mean nothing, but one finds those of Thackeray, Keen, and Browning, and in the room above the signatures of Walter Scott and Thomas Carlyle scratched on the window. No new names are allowed to be added. The back room, upstairs, contains the so-called "Stratford Portrait," now declared by Sidney Lee to have been painted from a bust in the eighteenth century. Below is the kitchen, one of the few rooms that has not been changed since the bard was a boy. Two rooms to the right are fitted up as a Museum, and contain early editions of the plays, portraits, and various relics. The Garden, at the back of the house, is filled with the trees and flowers mentioned in the plays.

Passing along High Street we see the house in which Judith, the daughter of the poet, lived for thirty-six years. Further on stands the picturesque half-timbered Harvard House, once the home of Katharine Rodgers, mother of John Harvard, founder of Harvard University. On Chapel Street is the site of New Place, the house in which the poet resided when he returned to Stratford, and where he died. Only the foundation remains. Opposite New Place is the old Guild Hall, where the boy may have seen troops of strolling players perform; in the upper story of which was the Grammar School which he attended. At the end of Church Street, we turn into the Old Town road which brings us to the Trinity Church, almost hidden amid trees on the bank of the Avon.

As we entered the Church, two aeroplanes passed over the town, like huge birds. I wondered what Shakespeare would have said. Be sure that fertile fancy, in which Ariel had his birth, would have found a phrase to fit the fact. The Church is interesting in itself, and in its treasures of art, but chiefly, of course, for that it is the tomb of the greatest genius of the English race. As Washington Irving said of it long of old, "The mind refuses to dwell on anything that is not connected with Shakespeare. His idea pervades the place; the whole pile seems but as his mausoleum. The feelings no longer checked by doubt, here indulge in perfect confidence; other traces of him may be false or dubious, but here is palpable evidence and absolute certainty."

Standing by that Grave on the north side of the chancel, I had such a sense of the reality of Shakespeare as I never had before. There, only a few feet below me, lay the actual dust of the Magician himself-divine dust, because his celestial spirit lent it Divinity, revealing all the heights and depths, the tragedy and comedy of this our mortal life. Who can pause beside that grave and doubt the triumph of the soul over death? How could that creative mind, that busy heart, cease to be? It is unthinkable! Only two other spots on earth have touched me with a like sense of the reality of immortality: one is Westminster Abbey, and the other is the grave of Emerson in Sleepy Hollow. As I read the oft-quoted epitaph with its warning, I thought, instead, of that wonderful 146th Sonnet, in which he conquered death before he died.

Nor must we forget the Memorial Theatre, that treasure-house of paintings of the Dramatist and his characters, which is also a library of Shakespearian books. From the top of the tower, reached by flights of steps and ladders, one sees another picture never to be forgotten. The town, the winding Avon, the summer beauty on the hills, it is as lovely as a dream. On one side of the theatre was a park, half full of men wearing the blue-gray uniform of wounded English soldiers, reminding us of the vast tragedy not far away. On the other side stands the Monument, erected in 1888 by Lord Gower, crowned with a giant image of the Poet, surrounded by figures representing Tragedy, History, Comedy, Philosophy.

Of course, we saw the Fountain, the gift of an American in 1887, in honor of the genius of Shakespeare and the jubilee of Queen Victoria. On our way, we met Marie Corelli out for an airing, a fat, chubby little lady she is, quite unlike her pictures. Reluctantly, with mingled joy and regret, we took the train for London. Always it is back to London, as of old all roads led to Rome. Now I know what the poet meant in his Rhymes of the Road,

"Go where you may, rest where you will,

Eternal London haunts you still."

PRAYER IS TRUST

The first great element of prayer is aspiration, a hunger for better being and doing, a looking onward and upward to an ideal which, seen afar off, is yearned after; a discontent with present attainments and performances, an inability to rest in things as they are. When a young man gives up wild or careless habits, begins to save money, to use his time to good account, brace himself against the lure to idleness and evil, he is praying, though he might be abashed if one told him that his wistful reaching forth toward something higher and better was prayer. Wherever improvement is being desired and sought, improvement not only in what we have, but in what we are and do, there is prayer, even though no word is uttered. A man in his workshop, factory or office, who, from morn to eve is striving to realize his ideal of honor, efficiency and service, is praying the livelong day. When an ideal of manhood is cherished, in the light of which our best is never wholly satisfactory, and which is evermore urging us to go beyond it, there is prayer. Such a man, though he kneel not during the day, goes prayerfully to his bed a better man, and the hum of his honest industry is the music of a liturgy.

Nor does he pray simply for himself alone. All prayer, by its very nature, is benevolent and intercessory. When a man is devoted to the pursuit of knowledge, caring more for it than for any worldly honor; when he is in search for truth, ready, if need be, to suffer that he may find it; when he desires to help forward a good cause, willing to sacrifice for it, when a man lives thus, he is exemplifying that love of the best things of which all prayer is the expression. Who can labor for the good and not begin to throb with desire for the good of others? What man, not cursed with hopeless selfishness, can enter the presence of the Eternal Goodness and ask only in his own behalf? When he closes the door of his oratory he remembers not simply his own burdens, but the griefs and woes of others. One who, like Abou Ben Adhem, loves his fellow man, need not bow his head and clasp his hands, before sleeping, to save the day from being prayerless, since it has been full of prayer. Yet no one can enter his oratory before falling into the mystery of sleep, without learning something for the comfort of his heart and the health of his soul.

Again, all true prayer has its roots in trust, and he is praying who dares trust truth, right, and honor, no matter the cost, though he may not kneel in a temple. Let him bow in the temple, but when on the day following, he obeys the light within him when it points, maybe, to a lonely road, where he will no longer walk with troops of friends, that also is prayer. If prayer is trust, he who trusts the reigning rectitude, trusts conscience, trusts duty, trusts principle habitually, fearful only of unfaithfulness, and with tranquil courage pursues his way, is a man of prayer. No matter how loud he may pray in the temple, if he seeks even a worthy end by unworthy means, his prayer has no wings. We pray by our desires, our motives, our tears. And by our acts, praying without ceasing to the God who is over all, in all, and working through all.

"THE SWORD OF AMERICA"

"My sword shall be bathed in heaven." - Isaiah xxiv. 5.

ALL through the Bible, the sword is a symbol of power, sometimes of a power used for evil ends, sometimes, more often indeed, for noble ends. The great watchword of the ancient Commonwealth in its trial, "The sword of the Lord and Gideon," might be used as a text for what the Bible has to say about the sword. Now, power is neither good nor evil; it is neutral. The purpose for which it is used, the spirit in which it is used, gives it moral quality. A bomb may be used to blow up a building, or to blast a tunnel for a railway opening new lands and inviting to new adventures. There are those who think that the use of any kind of force is wrong if it be used in behalf of moral and spiritual ends. Not at all. Force, used righteously in behalf of righteousness, is a sword of the Lord.

So, at least, Americans think of it, and with a few winsome and ardent exceptions, they are quite unanimous in feeling that the cause in behalf of which America and her allies fight is the cause of simple justice, decency, and mercy upon the earth. For the beautiful Quaker tradition, America has great respect, and should have respect. When the Quaker laid aside his great hat and drab coat and picked up his axe, he laid the foundation of some of the finest things in American life and literature. But in our wars of former times, if the Quaker was not permitted by his scruples actually to fight, he has always been a faithful servant of the Republic. Take our good, grey poet, Walt Whitman, who was of Quaker origin, as Lincoln was on one side of his family. He could not enter the ranks and take a gun and fight, but he entered the hospitals, and his service is memorable to this day in our annals. But for the man who will not render any service to his country because it is at war and he perchance may be lending some countenance to the existence of war, Americans can have very little respect. Conscience then sinks to the level of mere crankery. Such a person is not the object of scorn, but of pity. To such conscientious objectors, then America objects on conscientious grounds. She holds it to be true that no man has a moral right to the enjoyment or protection of a country whose institutions he will not support, and whose existence he will not defend. Let us be as true to Christianity as our sinful nature will allow us, and the grace of God will help us to be, but let us not identify Christianity with moral insanity.

Why did America hesitate to enter the war? Of course, I do not ask you to approve the reason, I only ask you to understand it. Washington, in his farewell address, told his country to keep clear of all entangling alliances with Europe. Why? Europe was at that time practically a monarchy from end to end. America, as Lincoln stated later, was conceived in liberty and dedicated to the proposition that all men are created equal. Therefore, the first President thought it wise for the Republic to live aloof for a time until it should be firmly established. His advice was wise; it was followed, and became the basis of all our national policy for more than a century. Now a century of national policy cannot be reversed overnight, it cannot be changed in a moment. But times change, and men change with them. Europe is no longer autocratic. Our enemies are trying to hold the last fortress of autocracy, and it must go. Europe is democratic, and it will be increasingly so in days to come. Therefore, the very reason why our country kept clear from entangling alliances with Europe in other days, for the same reason it has come into the fellowship of European nations.

America, then, has not simply entered the war, she has entered the world, reversing her whole national policy and the tendencies of her history, and this meant a complete revolution of thought and feeling in the Republic. In that connection, let me recall the words from a letter of Jefferson to Monroe in 1823:

"Great Britain is the nation which can do us the most harm of any one, or all, on earth; and with her on our side we need not fear the whole world. With her, then, we should sedulously cherish a cordial friendship; and nothing would tend more to knit our affections than to be fighting once more, side by side, in the same cause."

Today those words are fulfilled before our eyes, not because we fear harm from England, or have reason to suspect any threat from her, but because at last the policy of national isolation having become obsolete in America, and America having entered the world, her nearest neighbor is her Motherland. Today, the sons of the great Republic are fighting side by side with the sons of the great Empire.

What this will mean in the future, no one may venture to predict. Personally, I feel, and I believe, it is also the growing sentiment of my countrymen, that it is the outstanding fact connected with the whole tragedy of the war, and will have more influence on the future than any other event. If I should state my own conviction it would be after this manner:

"An alliance of the United States and the British Commonwealth on clearly defined terms of unquestionable explicitness, made in the open light of day, so that those planning aggression could realize clearly the formidable obstacle in their path, would effectively, though not absolutely, secure the general peace of the future world."

Such being the reason why America hesitated to enter the war, let me ask, in the second place, why she did enter the war? She was not indifferent; she was not incapable of moral indignation, as some of you may have felt. Why did we enter the war? Because our citizens had been assassinated on the high seas in ruthless barbarity? No, though that were cause enough if citizenship is to have meaning and value. Because we endured one unparalleled insult after another, such as perhaps no great and proud people had endured before? No. A rapscallion cannot insult a gentleman. Did we go to war, then, because our hospitality had been used for every conceivable kind of plot, involving our own people as well as the people of other nations, like a huge spider spinning its dark web of lying and spying all over the earth? No, though the discovery of those plots has made us very angry. America kept out of the war until she learned that the government of Germany is an organized lie. When she learned that, there was no other appeal but to the awful court of war.

Let me read you some words from Edmund Burke, the more so that he was a great champion of America, in the House of Commons, at the time of the war of the Revolution, and, of course, I need not say that America now understands that the reason for that war was that the King of England then was a German, and made a mess of things, as Germans usually do, those great words from the "Reflections on the French Revolution," one of the noblest passages in all political literature:

"Society is indeed a contract. It is a partnership in all science; a partnership in all art; a partnership in all virtue, and in all perfection. As the ends of such a partnership cannot be obtained in many generations, it becomes a partnership not only between those who are living, but between those who are living and those who are dead, and those who are to be born. Each contract of each particular state is but a clause in the great primeval contract of eternal society, linking the lower with the higher natures, connecting the visible with the invisible world, according to a fixed compact sanctioned by the inviolable oath which holds all physical and all moral natures, each in their appointed place."

Our enemies have violated the primeval contract of eternal society, making a treaty a "scrap of paper." An unwillingness to keep any national engagement that did not entirely suit their whim, throwing to the winds all moral obligation, is a violation of the contract on which all human society rests. Consider what would happen in London if a portion of its population decided to live according to a law of its own, to keep engagements only when it was convenient for them to do so; to respect obligations only when it was altogether pleasant and involved no sacrifice. What kind of community would there be in London? Law would vanish; business would collapse; anarchy would reign. What is true of one community is true the world over, and it was this violation of the primeval contract of society which arrayed the moral indignation of the world against Germany and her allies and drew America into the conflict.

For the same reason, there can be no peace, no negotiation looking towards peace, with the present German government. No treaty of peace signed by it is worth the paper on which it is written. It would be treated as lightly and as carelessly and as indifferently as other treaties have been treated. For that reason, America has not only gone into the war solemnly, deliberately, reluctantly, but she has gone into the war for profound moral and religious reasons. And for the same reasons, she will remain in it to the end and beyond, to see that the fundamental decencies of life are kept upon the earth, and that civilized society shall not perish.

Now, it is not possible for me in the time that remains to tell you what America in war-time is like. It is a grand and solemn thing to see a great nation mobilize all its forces, industrial, financial, moral, intellectual, spiritual, and prepare for a great contest. Never in our whole history has our Republic been so united, so cemented as it is today. In no other war has there been such a firm faith and clear and fixed conviction, not only of the righteousness of it, but of the necessity for it. I do not even except the war of the Revolution. I certainly do not except the Civil War. It means much, then, to have the moral judgment of a hundred millions of people. Our enemies have ignored these imponderable things. That is their greatest shame and their surest defeat. These things may seem to be intangible, but they are mighty; if they move slowly, they move surely, and history thunders in our ears telling us where they are going. Our enemies thought that the British Empire would fall to pieces, but instead the solidity and solidarity of the Empire has been revealed as in an apocalypse. They thought that America would remain indifferent, or could be frightened, but that was another blunder. Truly, it has been said that our enemies will go down in history as a people who foresaw everything except what actually happened, and who calculated everything except what it cost themselves.

From the Rocky Mountains in the Far West; from the great prairies of the Middle West; from the valleys and forests of the South; down out of the stony hills of New England; up from the great Central States, come young men marching, marching, marching, most of them having volunteered, most of the States having filled up their quota by volunteer enlistment before the draft came into effect. These young men come from all walks of life, our universities and colleges especially giving their very best, some of them being quite depopulated. They march with one step, and they sing one song. It is quite different from the war with Spain in one particular, there is very little noise; there is a quietness that is rather unusual in America, and which is for that reason easily mistaken as to its meaning. I should like to speak a word particularly about the Middle West, which English people do not understand at all. It has been quiet; we have made very little noise out in the Middle West, but the Middle West and the South are the most American parts of America. Out there men do not say: "Let somebody else go and do it" they go themselves. So, when it came to the matter of enlisting, when it came to furnishing funds for the great Liberty Loan, the Middle West was in the van and led the way.

Let me also say something about our fellow citizens of German origin. Perhaps 85 or 90 percent of them are as loyal and true-hearted in their devotion to the Republic as any other class of citizens. They are not pro-English, they are not pro-French, but they are pro-American. They came, or their fathers came before them, to America, to get away from the hideous, hateful thing that has turned Germany into what it is today. They hate the Kaiser and all his works. They love America. They were attracted to America by its idealism, its opportunity for development. Karl Schurz was typical of this large class. You have read of his flight from Germany, of his short stay in England, of his journey to America, where he climbed from the bottom to the top and became a member of the Senate. A very able and noble man he was. When he returned to Germany, he took pains to tell Bismarck of the difference between living in a Republic and living in an autocracy. You may find it in his "Conversations with Bismarck," after this manner: Living in an autocracy is like riding on a great ocean liner. All the appointments are perfect, but you have nothing to do with running the boat. The details are quite satisfactory, but the general direction is wrong. Living in a democracy is like riding on a raft or a flatboat. The passengers get their feet wet, they take cold, and they sneeze. They have an uncomfortable time, but they run the boat, and they know where it is going.

These people sympathize deeply with the folk of their own blood in the Fatherland, but they have no sympathy with the German Government or that for which it stands. There is a small minority, perhaps 10 percent of late comers to America, attracted not by its idealism but by its opportunities to make money, who have not yet become American. For I take it that an American is a man who holds in his heart as sacred that for which America stands, no matter what his race or religion may be. And America is not a new England, it is not a new Europe, it is a new world. It is founded upon a principle to which it has been true through these years, to build a nation not for the rich, though its resources may make men rich, not for the elect, who can make their way anywhere or everywhere; but a nation where the plain common man can stand erect, can stretch his arms and his soul and be free; own his home; cast his vote and have his voice in the affairs of the State. That small minority of Germans who have not yet become American have made a good deal of noise, have acted very unwisely, aided by propagandists from the Home Country, but Americans know how to deal with them. Either of three things will happen, or all three: they will be interned, their property will be confiscated, and at the close of the war they will be deported back to the Germany of which they are so fond.

Not lightly did America go into the war, offering her bravest and her best to stand side by side with your bravest and best. The mingling of our common blood in a common sacrifice means the consecration of us all. We must renew our vows, our high and holy determination that the Britain for which Britons have fought so valiantly, with such superhuman courage, the America for which young Americans are now to fight, shall in the future be a greater, better Britain, a greater, purer America. Back across the years come the words of Lincoln in the hour of our national crisis, which express today the feeling of his country in a greater time of trial, these words:

"Fondly do we hope, fervently do we pray that this mighty scourge of war may speedily pass away. Yet if God wills that it continue, as was said 3000 years ago, so still it must be said, 'The judgments of the Lord are true and righteous altogether.' With malice toward none, with charity for all, with firmness in the right as God gives us to see the right, let us strive on to finish the work we are in; to bind up the nation's wounds; to care for him who shall have borne the battle, and for his widow and his orphan; to do all which many achieve and cherish a just and lasting peace among ourselves and with all nations."

"My sword shall be bathed in Heaven," in heavenly principles, in a heavenly spirit. So far as we in America are concerned, it is not a war of hate. It is not a war of revenge; we have no old scores to clear off. It is not a war of conquest, we do not want an inch of land from any people. But we realize that Europe cannot be free, America cannot be free, that no free institution can be safe, until the military autocracy of Prussia is crushed, and to that one end we unite with you, heart and hand and soul, that the future may be safer and nobler for your children and for ours.

Our philosophy of patriotism is that each nation has, by the gift of God, something unique, particular and precious; something not to be found anywhere else, and therefore it has a gift to make to universal humanity. That it may make that gift it should be free to develop what is most unique and precious in its life. Therefore, we say to our enemies: "We will not impose our culture upon any other people, and you shall not impose your kultur upon any other people." Kultur! The very word stinks to the stars. We do not want an internationalism that is a mere abstraction, that bleaches out all our local loyalties and human heroisms. Not at all; just as in religion, we do not want unity of the churchyard, we want the unity of the Church, unity with variety, the unity of a flower garden, where there is one soil and one air, and every variety of color, so we want an international understanding that shall permit each nation to develop, not a narrow bigoted nationalism, but shall give to all what is most precious and holy in its life. To do that it must be free. For that it is that America is fighting, seeking the Excalibur that King Arthur found at last. When he was beaten and broken and wounded and his sword was of no further use, in the enchanted lake he saw the white arm of a woman holding a sword, the most excellent sword of right, with which he had vanquished his foes. The name of that sword was truth, its sheath was faith.

AN AMBASSADOR

UNFORTUNATELY, I have had to neglect my duties as Ambassador of late, or at least to omit my reports, for which I beg forgiveness. The fact is that I have been spending every odd hour in the great military camps, speaking to the men, visiting with them, and seeing something of their life. My work has been chiefly among Canadians and Americans, our New World men who are the finest in the world, such erect, upstanding fellows they are, too, clear-cut, forthright, with something of the large, free and liberal air of the fogless spaces of North America.

In one thing, the Canadians are ahead of us. They have organized camp colleges, where their men, many of them, like our own, college men, continue their studies, for which they receive due credit in the colleges and universities at home. They are real colleges, too. I have visited two of them, to deliver addresses at the close of a term, and I find them doing thorough work, especially in science and agriculture and the more practical branches. Naturally, the literary side is not so much emphasized, but it is by no means neglected. These colleges, of course, have the approval of the authorities, not only approval, but encouragement, and I see no reason why our people should not wake up to the possibilities of such a work.

Two days ago, I went to speak to the great American camp, the name and location of which I must not give too accurately. It was a delight to see those boys, who are so responsive to all high things. I spoke in a large moving-picture theatre, which was packed and jammed; then it was emptied, only to be filled again, and I talked another hour. They actually did it a third time, and by the end of the third hour I was "all in," as you can imagine. Another crowd was waiting, but I was not equal to the task. They are from all over the Union, from Texas to New York, and a more wholesome set of boys I never saw in my life. Not only physically, but morally, which is quite as important in war, they are admirably cared for by those in command.

Among those in the camp I visited were the survivors of the Tuscania, and it was good to see men who had gone through that ordeal. And funny, too, for they were togged out in every kind of rig, by the kindness of a camp of English Tommies nearby, because those who did not lose their clothing, had it ruined by the sea-water. Hence their plight, awaiting the arrival of a new outfit. But they were in fine spirits. As one of them put it, they lost everything except their nerve, their courage, and their determination to get the scalps of the Huns. Indeed, the attack has put new iron into their blood and made them more anxious to have a "go" at the enemy.

LINKING ENGLAND AND AMERICA

PRESIDENT WILSON'S desire is to make the world "secure for democracy," to abolish the nightmare fear of sudden war, and with it the necessity for maintaining huge armies and navies. It is no selfish motive, for he wishes for the people whom he rules what they would eagerly and whole-heartedly share with all mankind.

At present, that high purpose is not only unaccomplished, but actually menaced with final disappointment. So far from hard-won democratic institutions being safe, they are at this moment in dire peril. They are in peril so great and urgent that a peace-loving people, separated from Europe by a thousand leagues of ocean, still cherishing a tradition inherited from Washington and Franklin of non-intervention in the quarrels of the Old World, feel that duty, religion, honor, and humanity bid them take up arms and wage war with all their might against a soulless autocracy which threatens to enslave the world.

This seems to me the greatest event of modern times, because, if it be crowned with success, as we believe it will be, it may well inaugurate a new era, the Era of Settled Peace. And not only or chiefly because the "men that delight in war" have been subdued, but because the association of Britain and America in this great and holy cause is likely to eradicate, to uproot the last vestige of remembrance of the quarrel which separated them.

That quarrel has long ago been virtually forgotten in Britain. But American history begins not with Julius Caesar, but with George Washington, not with the Battle of Hastings, but with a revolution, which resulted in thirteen British colonies, hitherto passionately loyal, taking the style and title of the United States of America; not with Magna Charta, but with that Declaration of Independence, the signing of which is the chief landmark in the American citizen's historical landscape.

The boys and girls read of these things in the earliest pages of their school-books. Bunker Hill and Lexington become magical names to them. First impressions being lasting, grown-up Americans have been apt to forget it was a German king, George the Third, opposed by the best and noblest of his advisers, and contrary to the wishes of the people of Britain, whose blind obstinacy and congenital insanity drove the American colonies into revolt.

Yes, and they are also apt to forget, whilst knowing speeches of Franklin, Webster and Lincoln by heart, the words thundered by Pitt in the British House of Commons: "I rejoice that America has resisted. Three millions of people so dead to all the feelings of liberty as voluntarily to submit to be slaves, would have been fit instruments to make slaves of the rest."

Today, those three millions have become one hundred millions. Yet, mark the miracle, America is still but a larger Britain across the ocean. From Atlantic to Pacific, she speaks the tongue of Shakespeare and Bunyan; her public and private life is based on English custom; her traditions and literature are one with the Motherland; her ideals of civilization, those of the isle from which her Pilgrim Fathers sailed.

Furthermore, America's greatest church was founded by Wesley, an Oxford clergyman; her two leading universities, Yale and Harvard, by Englishmen; every president she has elected, except two, has borne a British surname. Her laws are confessedly founded on English law, and the usages and precedents of the courts in the two countries are almost identical. Her ideas of liberty, justice, and freedom, for conscience, for the individual, for the

Press, are the ideas promulgated by the great Puritans, Cromwell, Hampden, Milton, and Bunyan.

In short, the influence upon the fundamental life of America of all other nations combined is negligible compared with the profound and ineradicable influence of Britain.

Then how greatly desirable is a sympathetic and intelligent understanding between these two kindred peoples. Neither nation has taken sufficient pains to understand the other. Superficial differences have been able to obscure fundamental unities.

But in the furnace of this world war, upon the anvil of a common and noble purpose, under the hammer, kindred peoples will be rewelded, and then in their keeping chiefly will be the future of mankind.

And who can doubt that the heart-union of the British Empire and the United States of America means for the world an era of unbroken Peace in which service and not enslavement, enlightenment and not exploitation, artsy, hearts and not arms will be the watchword of statesmen and rulers? Certainly, all who help forward this great friendship are thereby laboring for the better future of humanity.

A LEAGUE OF MASONS

IN my office as Ambassador I have the honor to transmit herewith, through the Research Society, to the Masons of America a message truly memorable in Masonic annals, and which will command the attention of brethren of every jurisdiction. The distinction of its author, Worshipful Brother Sir Alfred Robbins, the high office of President of the Board of General Purposes of the Grand Lodge of England which he has held for so many years, its vision of "English and American Brotherhood," its gracious spirit, its lofty tone, all these set it apart as a document unique in our literature, and prophetic of a closer fellowship in the days to be. It is a pleasure to have suggested such an article; it is an honor to spread it before the Masons of America, who will not fail to respond to its brotherly spirit and its historic meaning.

Surely, in a world torn by strife, and divided by so many feuds of race, religion and nationality we have a right to rejoice in a fellowship, at once free, gentle and refining, which spans all distances of space and all differences of speech, and brings men together by a common impulse and inspiration in mutual respect and brotherly regard. It needs no prophet to discern that such a fraternity, the very existence of which is a fact eloquent beyond words, is an influence for good to which we can set pro limit, and a prophecy for the future the meaning of which no one can measure; doubly so now, because, by its genius, Masonry is international, and therefore ought to be responsive to the ideal of world-fellowship which will surely emerge from the welter of the world-war.

For that reason, in the reunion of English-speaking peoples, upon which the future freedom and peace of the world so much depend, among the many ties of language, literature, love of liberty, respect for law, social institutions and historic inheritance, that unite us, must be counted a common and great Freemasonry. By the same token, upon our Fraternity rests an obligation only equaled by the opportunity, to have a far-reaching part in promoting fellowship, interpretation and sympathetic and intelligent understanding between two peoples in whose history it is so deeply interwoven, and of whose unity it is itself a tie, a token, and a prophecy. Our differences are superficial; our unities fundamental. Such variations as exist between English and American Masonry, like the differences between the two peoples, are interesting, albeit insignificant, no more important than the variations of accent and inflection, of dialect and brogue; its basic truths and principles are alike, and its spirit is the same in its breadth, beauty, and benignity.

If there is to be a League of Nations following the war, such a federation of free peoples as shall make the repetition of this disaster impossible, it should begin with a league of English-speaking peoples who have one historic faith, one conception of civilization, and one political ideal. Looking toward that consummation so devoutly to be wished, how better can we begin than by seeking to realize a League of Masons, such as Sir Alfred Robbins suggests; the more so because it is the declared purpose of our Craft to labor for a league of mankind, which it seeks even now to exhibit on a small scale. Freemasonry, by virtue of its exalted purpose, its high intellectual quality, its noble morality, and its wise spirituality, ought to lead the way toward that City of Equity which poets and prophets have seen afar off adown the ages.

For, to say no more, our English-speaking race, by its spirit, its genius, its history, no less than by its great Freemasonry, is committed to the ideal of a Commonwealth, the application to the field of government and social policy of the law of human brotherhood, the duty of man to his neighbor, near and far, wherein lies our only hope of a world fit for free men to live in, where maternity can flourish and the spirit of good will can grow and be glorified.

THE COMMON GOOD

ONE OF THE supreme needs of our time, as its deepest thinkers agree, is a conception of the Common Good worthy of our human enterprise; the perception that the good of humanity as a whole actually exists, not as a dream, but as a reality, and that the good of any race, nation or class can only be realized in the community of interest and obligation. For that reason, the ancient word is as true today as it was ages ago, and as true of a nation as of an individual: "Who seeks his own loses the things in common."

In one of his poems William Morris speaks of the problems of our day as a "tangled wood," until they are seen in the light of life's meaning as a whole, and "looking up, at last we see The glimmer of the open light, From o'er the place where we would be: Then grow the very brambles bright."

Many great seers and thinkers have looked up seeking the meaning of life, the goal of its uprising passion and desire, the purpose of its organization in the home, in the state, in industry, in moral fellowship and spiritual faith; and thus have tried to point the way out of the "tangled wood" in which we wander.

Plato dreamed of an ideal Republic but his vision no longer satisfies us, because of its stratification of society into castes. There is the Augustinian vision of the City of God, written when the Eternal City was reeling to its fall, not to name our modern Utopias of many and various kinds, in which we see the human mind trying to form a worthy conception of the goal of human development. But all these dawns are dwarfed by the ideal that shone in the mind of the man of Galilee, to whom we owe a vision equal, alike in its nobility and grandeur, to our human undertaking. In nothing did the gentle Teacher more assuredly reveal His greatness than in His amazing faith in the communal redemption of humanity; His vision of mankind living by the law of love in a Beloved Community here, now, upon earth. He called it the Kingdom of Heaven, and He exhausted the resources of His incomparable speech, fresh as the dew and bright with color, to make it real and vivid to men.

If the same ideal be set forth in the symbolism of Freemasonry, it is a vision of a living Temple, noble, stately, sheltering all the holy things of humanity, slowly rising in the midst of the ages; a Temple building and built upon, each workman not only a builder, but himself a living stone, foursquare and finely wrought, to be built into the whole; each generation of builders adding an arch, a pillar, or a spire, as the grey old cathedrals were uplifted, strong and piteous, matching the masonry of the mountains in their grandeur, each race of Masons building upon the foundations laid by their vanished comrades. In height, in depth, in breadth and beauty it is the noblest vision that has come within sight of our groping human mind, in that it flashes before even the dullest mind a vision of something immortal, a sequence of aim and obligation, of cooperative fellowship, which annuls the ephemeral and reveals the eternal in time.

Such must be our insight and faith, if our fraternal sentiment is not to evaporate in misty eloquence, or else be only a rope of sand; the faith that we are fellow workers with the eternal Creative Goodwill, and therefore made to be not only Builders but Brothers, made to share the large innocence of nature and the unfailing love of God who cares more for a brother than for all possessions; and that if we do not live after the law of our highest nature, a veil falls over the beauty of the world, leaving us to wander alone or to struggle together in confusion and strife. For, if we are to have a philosophy, much less an ethic, of fraternity we must learn "that goodness is not merely some form of similar activity of self and neighbor, but is really an attitude of each to the other; the realization, indeed, of spiritual kinship and unity," in short, that goodness is community, fellowship, mutuality, and that it takes two men and God to make a brother.

More specifically, as the world now stands, we are faced by four great and urgent issues, if our civilization is to endure, much less fulfil its beneficent mission. Each of these issues demands a commanding vision of the Common Good, each is a challenge to the practical brotherliness of humanity, and if we are to meet them, we must not lose "the glimmer of the open light." First, and chiefly, we must organize the goodwill of the world and make an end of war, otherwise war will leave the Temple of Man a charred and smoking ruin, as it has well-nigh done today. Second, we must meet the threat of a corrosive anarchy with a profounder sense of communal fellowship and obligation, in which each counts for one and nobody for more than one, joined with a sense of the sanctity of the common will expressed in law, order, and the fair humanities of society.

Third, so long as distances were great, and races lived far apart, friction was not keenly felt, but today the world has shrunk to the size of a neighborhood and many races mingle. Inter-racial relations will be an acute and vital matter in the days that lie ahead of us, doubly so in our Republic where one feels always the presence of racial suspicion. As a welter of rancors, as a wrangle of irritations it is hopeless; only brotherliness can solve it. Fourth, the tangle of industrial unrest is hopeless if its issues are left to be fought over by extremists, and the struggle may shatter a society already cracked by the shock of world-war, here, again, there is no hope save in a gradual deepening of communal interest and responsibility, until, at last, private interest and vested interest are subordinate to the Common Good. Inevitably, in the long last, the common good will replace selfish interest as the ruling motive, even in the market-place, as necessity dictated during the war.

Henceforth, we must measure and interpret all human activities and institutions as they stand in the service of the Common Good; as they are related to the Temple whose builders we are. Not alone the Lodge, but the Church, the State, the Home, the organization of life in art, in science, in industry, in moral endeavor and immortal hope, have here their sanction and consecration. Not otherwise may we know the worth and meaning of our individual lives, so brief, so broken, so be shadowed, save as we see them in the fellowship of the large purpose of the Master Builder. So, and only so, are we redeemed from insignificance and futility, and our fleeting days endowed with epic power and prophecy. It is when we enlist as the fellow-workers of the Eternal that life reveals its own eternal quality, and we learn the final answer to all pessimisms, all cynicisms, and all skepticisms whatsoever.

The New Age stands as yet
Half built against the sky,
Open to every threat
Of storms that clamor by.
Scaffolding veils the walls
And dim dust floats and falls
As moving to and fro, their tasks
The Masons ply.

THE MYSTIC TIE

"The moral solidarity of mankind is dissolved. The danger is imminent that the end may be a war of all against all. Sects and parties are increasing; common estimates and ideals keep slipping away; we understand one another less and less; even voluntary associations, that form of unity peculiar to modern times, unite more in accomplishment than disposition, bring men together outwardly rather than in reality."

These words, written by Rudolph Eucken in 1912, were like a star-shell over No Man's Land, revealing the divided mind of the world, and they had a terrible fulfilment. The War, by its principle of violence, made no positive contribution to society, but only stirred up and brought to the surface what already existed. For both men and nations, it intensified tendencies already active, precipitated passions held in obscure solution, and brought to a focus forces that had long been uneasily accumulating. It neither initiated nor changed the direction in which the world was moving, but it did quicken the pace, and, in quickening it, revealed it. That is why a haunting uneasiness possesses the minds of men today. Even when local disturbances subside and isolated disputes are settled, we still doubt whether a stable tranquility has returned or ever will return again. For these things are only symptoms of a profound and widespread mental ferment and moral restlessness.

The insight of Eucken goes further back and deeper down to the real root of the matter, divining the causes and logic of it all to be moral, spiritual, religious. For, if anything is made plain by history, it is that the mystic tie which holds humanity together in ordered and advancing life is moral and spiritual, and when that thread is cut anything may happen. From the beginning of the century, the spiritual disintegration of the modern world, the breaking of the ties that bind together the fabric of civilization, had been observed and noted by many. Faith grew dim, moral sanctions were relaxed, and it was deemed clever and smart to talk lightly of those sanctities without which no society has long existed. Much of our literature has been intellectually Bolshevistic for thirty years, attacking the basis of marriage, of the home, of the church, of the state, as if the moral laws were only conventions, if not fictions. Verily, we have our reward; we know now that when fools play with fire they get burned.

For a time, during the stress and strain and terror of the war, there seemed to be a reknitting of the ties that bind men and nations together; but it was only seeming. It was the power of fear and force, not the power of faith. How unreal, how artificial it was is shown by the rapidity with which that amazing solidarity was demobilized, to be followed by a revival of class rancor, sectarian ardor, and a narrow, myopic nationalism. A world which, having sent young men to die by the thousands for magnanimous ideals, has already half-forgotten them as it cooly and briskly resumes business at the old stand, such a world may be grieved, but it ought not to be astonished, at the revolt of both the minds and souls of men. Not that the immediate future will see a triumph of subversive schemes and radical ideas. If we follow an almost universal precedent, we shall pass first through a period of luxury and extravagance, and there will be a momentary craving for the old social and religious orders, as in the years following the Napoleonic Wars. But this is not significant. It is merely the first reaction from the emotional strain and nervous tension of the war. This mood will soon spend itself, and then, at once, new forms, new forces, new demands will begin to arise which will sweep away much that has seemed precious and permanent in our lives.

Without a spiritual renewal, without a reknitting of that "moral solidarity," of which Eucken speaks so eloquently, without the Mystic Tie, we may not hope for security and real progress. The truth is that we have been trying to build a human civilization on a materialistic foundation, and it cannot be done. No human community can long exist on such a basis. Russia has rendered incalculable service to humanity, by showing, with deadly consistency, how materialism issues into anarchy and animalism. Hear now a proof of this in the words of a spiritually-minded man who lived in the midst of it, watching the decay and destruction of his country. Eugene Troubetzkoy, Professor of Law in the University of Moscow, in the Hibbert Journal, for January, 1920, shows us what happens when the tie of spiritual faith and fellowship is broken. Here are words which he who runs may read:

"Bolshevism is first and foremost the practical denial of the spiritual. They flatly refuse to admit the existence of any spiritual bond between man and man. For them, economic and material interests constitute the only social nexus; they recognize no other. This is the source of their whole conception of human society. The love of country, for example, is a lying hypocritical pretense; for the national bond is a spiritual bond, and therefore wholly fictitious. From their point of view, the only real bond between men is the material, that is to say, the economic. Material interests divide men into classes, and they are the only divisions to be taken account of. Hence, they recognize no Nations save the Rich and the Poor. As there is no other bond which can unite these two Nations into one social whole, their relations must be regulated exclusively by the zoological principle revealed in the struggle for existence.

The materialistic conception of society is the Bolshevist method of treating the family. Since there is no spiritual bond between the sexes, there can be no constant relation. The rule is therefore, that men and women can change their partners as often as they wish. The authorities in certain districts have even proclaimed the 'nationalization' of women, that is, the abolition of any private and exclusive right to process a wife even for a limited period, on the ground that women are the property of all. The same with children. A powerful current of opinion is urging that children must be taken from their parents in order that the State may give them an education on true materialistic lines. In certain communes some hundreds of children were 'nationalized,' that is, 'taken from their parents and placed in public institutions."

There it is, showing us what the red logic of hell means when it works itself out in action, and what results follow when the Mystic Tie of spiritual faith and fellowship is cut. Political anarchy, social animalism, moral bedlam follow with mathematical certainty, and all the fine and holy things of life are thrown into the junk heap. Man has an animal inheritance, moods of ape and tiger mingle in him with divine dreams and thoughts that wander through eternity, and when the Divine is denied, he reverts to the law of the jungle, and the hard-won trophy of spiritual struggle and agony vanishes. What happens, happens again. The Bolshevists are men of like passions as ourselves; they simply carry out with the fatal logic of fanaticism the dogma of materialism upon which we have been trying to base our modern civilization. If anyone thinks that what has taken place in Russia cannot happen in America, he knows little of history and less of human nature. The practical denial of the Divine dehumanizes humanity, and the rest follows as night follows day.

For that reason, if it should be a part of our religion to be patriotic, it must be a part of our patriotism to keep the light of spiritual faith aflame on the altars built by our fathers. Down in Wales, at a time when it seemed that revolution was inevitable, I asked a labor leader what bond held men together. He said: "All that holds these men back is the fact that they were trained in the Sunday-schools of these Welsh chapels years ago. That is all that keeps the spark from blowing up." Within the last four years, ten thousand Sunday-schools have ceased to exist in America, and the end is not yet. Facts such as these, and others of like kind, make a thoughtful man wonder as to what the future will be. What confronts us is not specifically indifference to religion, but indifference to pretty well everything outside the circle of creature comfort and self-gratification. There are many exceptions, of course, but in the main it is true that society has as yet been able to persuade only a few of its members to be really interested in its higher concerns. By the same token, men who do care for what is finest in our national life must make use of every opportunity, every instrumentality, to keep alive the faith that makes men faithful, and the vision of the moral ideal that lights our human way toward the city of God.

There is no need to apply what has been said, least of all to men to whom the Mystic Tie is a reality, and who are bound together by it in a fraternity of spiritual Faith and Fellowship. In every degree of Freemasonry, we are taught by art, by drama, by symbol, the moral basis of human society, its spiritual interpretation, and the necessity of a fraternal righteousness among men, without which manhood is rudimentary and intellectual culture is the slave of greed and passion. Of Lincoln it was said, that "his practical life was spiritual," and by as much as Masonry builds men of like faith and fiber who, in private life and public service, keep a manhood neither bought nor sold, true of heart and unbefogged of mind, it is helping to weave that Mystic Tie that holds the republic together. The words of James Bryce, in "The American Commonwealth," ought to be written and hung up in our hearts:

"If history teaches anything, it teaches us that hitherto civilized society has rested on religion. It was religious zeal and religious conscience that led to the founding of the New England colonies two centuries and a half ago. Religion and conscience have been a constantly active force in the American Commonwealth ever since. And the more democratic republics become, the more the masses grow conscious of their power, the more do they need to live not only by patriotism, but by reverence and self-control, and the more essential to their well-being are those sources from which reverence and self-control flow."

THE MENS HOUSE

(This address was first given in the form of a sermon to a company of Masons.)

AFTER all, the great secret of Masonry is that it has no secret, and might better be called the Open Secret of the World. If it retires into the tyled recesses of the lodge and works in the quiet and privacy thereof, it is the better to teach in parable, symbol, emblem and drama those great and simple truths which are to our human world what light and air are to the natural world. When a young man enters a Masonic lodge, he is asked whence he came, and what he has come to do. Today let us reverse that order of inquiry and ask of Masonry the question which she asks of all who bow at her altar: Whence it has come, and what service it has to render to humanity? Time does not allow us to answer such questions in detail, but perhaps a brief sketch may provoke others to pursue the study, and thus learn how far back the story of Masonry goes, and how deeply it is rooted in the nature, need and aspiration of the race.

In primitive society, there were four institutions, with three of which we are familiar, but the fourth is not so well known. There was, first of all, the most fundamental, the Home, the cornerstone of society and civilization. It was crude, as all things were in the morning of the world, yet it had in it the prophecy of that enshrinement of beauty and tenderness into which we were born, and the memory of which remains to consecrate us. There was the Temple of Prayer, not a temple at first, but only a rough altar of uncut stone, uplifted by the same instinct for the Eternal which built the great cathedrals. Its rites were rude, often grotesque and horrible, yet even in the darkness of a great Fear there were gleams of "that light that never was on sea or land" by which we are guided through the labyrinth of the world. Then there was the state, beginning in patriarchal rule, merging thence into the tribe and the nation, and at last we see many nations fused into huge empires which met in the clash of conflict. The state, too, was rude, but it had in it the rudiments of our patriotic devotion to our Republic.

EARLY SOCIETY SECRET

But there was another institution, quite as old as the other three and hardly less important, to which we are more indebted than we realize. Of this hidden institution, let me speak more in detail, not only for its human interest, but also for the fact that Masonry perpetuates it among us today. It was called the Men's House, a secret lodge in which every young man, when he came to maturity, was initiated into the law, legend, tradition and religion of his people. Recent research has brought to light this long hidden institution, showing that it was really the center of early tribal life, the council chamber, the guest house, and the meeting place of men where laws were made and courts were held, and where the trophies of war were treasured. Indeed, early society was really a secret society, and unless we keep this fact in mind, we can hardly understand it at all. It is the key to the interpretation of the evolution of primitive social life, and without it one can scarcely know the process of human development.

When tribal solidarity was more important than tribal expansion, it is hard to exaggerate the value of these lodges as providing bonds based upon feelings of kinship, and as promoting a sense of social unity and loyalty which lies at the root of law, order and religion. Methods of initiation differed in different times and places, but they had, nevertheless, a certain likeness, as they had always the same purpose. Ordeals often severe and sometimes frightful were required, exposing the initiate not only to physical torture, but also the peril of unseen spirits, as tests to prove youth worthy, by reason of virtue and valor, to be entrusted with the secret lore of his people. The ceremonies included vows of chastity, of courage, of secrecy and loyalty, and, almost always, a drama representing the advent of the novice into a new life. Moreover, the new life to which he awoke after his "initiation into manhood," for such it truly was, included a new name, a new language or signs, grips and tokens, and new privileges and responsibilities. If a youth failed to endure the tests, and proved to be a coward or a weakling, he became the scorn of every man of his tribe.

No doubt it was the antiquity of the idea and necessity of initiation which our Masonic fathers had in mind when they said that Masonry began with the beginning of history, and they were not so far wrong as certain smart folk think they were. At any rate, they saw clearly the service of secret societies in the development of civilization, and that, like the home and the temple, the Men's House was one of the great institutions of humanity. When the tribes ceased to be the unit of society, giving place to the nation, the secret training place for men became at once a school and temple, preserving and transmitting the truths of religion, the rudiments of science, and the laws of art, all of which were universally held as sacred secrets to be known only to the initiated. By a certain wise instinct, men felt that everything must not be told to everybody, but that men must approve themselves as worthy to receive truths which had cost so much; and that instinct was wise and true. Even the gentle Teacher of Galilee would not cast His pearls before swine, and it was therefore that He taught in parables, cryptic and dim. Hence the great ancient orders called the Mysteries, which ruled the world for ages before our era, and he who would estimate the spiritual possessions of humanity must take account of their influence and power. Thus, the Mysteries of Mithra in the East, of Isis in Egypt, and the Eleusian Mysteries of Greece swayed mankind, using every device of art to teach the truths of faith and hope and righteousness. In the temple of the Mysteries, which contained the tradition and ministry of the Men's House, the greatest men of antiquity received initiation, such men as Pythagoras, Plato, Plutarch, to name no others, and Cicero tells us that the truths taught in the house of the hidden place made men love virtue and gave them happy thoughts for the hour of death. Those temples of the Mysteries were shrines where art, philosophy, science and religion had their home, and from which, as time passed, they spread out fanwise along the avenue of human culture.

THE TEMPLE BUILDERS

History is no older than architecture. Man could not become a civilized being until he had learned to build a settled habitation, a Home for his family, a Temple for his faith, a Memorial for his dead. So, and naturally so, the Men's House came at last to be associated with the art of building, with the constructive genius of the race, using the laws and tools of the builder as emblems to teach the truths of faith and morality. Long before our era we find an order of Builders called the Dionysian Artificers, working in Asia Minor, where they erected temples, theatres and palaces, a secret order whose ceremonies perpetuated the ancient drama of the Mysteries, and they were almost certainly the builders of the Temple of Solomon. Thence we trace them eastward into India, and westward into Rome, where they were identified with the Roman College of Architects whose emblems have come down to us.

When Rome fell, a band of artists took refuge on a fortified island in Lake Como, in Northern Italy, where for a period they lived, offering an asylum to their persecuted fellows, and where they preserved the traditions of classic art. From them descended the great order of Comacine Masters, the Cathedral Builders, whom we can trace through the Middle Ages, and who early became known as Freemasons, free, because they were exempt from many restraints, and unlike Gild Masons, were permitted to travel at liberty wherever their work required. They were great artists, commanding the service of the finest intellects of the age, yet so bound together that, as Hallam said, no cathedral can be traced to any one artist. For the cathedrals were not the work of any one man, but the creation of a fraternity who so united the spirit of fraternity with a sense of the sanctity of art as to obliterate individual aggrandizement and personal ambition.

Thus, the Freemasons traveled through the years, building those monuments of beauty and prayer which still consecrate the earth, until the decline of Gothic architecture, when the order of Cathedral Builders began to decline. As early as 1600, scholars and students of mysticism began to ask to be accepted as members of lodges of Freemasons, the better to study their symbolism and teachings, as, for example, Ashmole, who founded the museum which bears his name at Oxford. These men though not actual architects, were accepted as members of the order, hence Free and Accepted Masons. From earliest time, as we may learn from our own Bible, as well as from many ancient writings, such as the Chinese classics and the Egyptian Book of the Dead, the tools and laws of building had been used as symbols of moral and spiritual truth; and when the work of practical architecture became so changed as no longer to require the service of a fraternal order, the Freemasons ceased to be builders of temples of brick and stone, but retained their organization and traditions, builders not less than before, but using their tools as symbols of the truths and principles with which they sought to build a Temple of Righteousness and Friendship upon earth.

FREEDOM, FRIENDSHIP, FRATERNITY

This newer Masonry, as it has been called, took form in the organization of the Grand Lodge of England, in 1717, from which it has descended to us having spread all over the civilized world. Forming one great society of devout and free men, it toils in every land in behalf of Freedom, Friendship and Fraternity among men, seeking to establish government without tyranny and religion without superstition; seeking, that is, to refine and exalt the lives of men, to purify their thought and ennoble their faith; teaching them to live and let live, to think and let think, to love peace and pursue it. Truly, the very existence of such an order of men, initiated, sworn and trained to uphold all the redeeming ideals of humanity, is an eloquent and far shining fact. It does not solicit members, save in so far as its influence in a community may invite the cooperation of right-thinking men who wish to foster what is noblest in humanity, toiling the while to strengthen that social and moral sentiment which gives to law its authority and to the gospel its sovereign opportunity.

What, then, is Masonry? For one thing, let it be said with all emphasis that it is in no sense a political society, and its historic Constitutions, called Old Charges, forbid the discussion of political issues in its lodges "as what never yet conduced to the welfare of the lodge, nor never will." Individual Masons, like others, have their political opinions; but as Masons, and certainly as a lodge of Masons, we never take part in political disputes. There was once an anti-Masonic political party in this country, born of falsehood and fed on fanaticism, which defeated Henry Clay for the presidency because he was a Mason;

but, without intending to do so, it elected Jackson, who was also a Mason. While Masonry is not a political order, for politics divides men, and it is the mission of Masonry to unite them, it does train men for citizenship, and it is a fact that it did in this way write its basic principles of civil and religious liberty into the organic law of this Republic. Our first President was a Master Mason, and was sworn into office on an open Bible taken from a Masonic altar.

Having presided over the birth of this Republic, the Masonic order has stood guard all down the years of its history, its altar lights along the heights of liberty; and so it will be to the end. Let it never be forgotten that, in an evil hour, when States were torn apart and churches were rent in two, the fellowship of Masonry remained unbroken, true and tender amidst the mad passion of civil war. If it was unable to prevent the strife, it did mitigate the horrors of it, building rainbow bridges from battle line to battle line. When this period of Masonic history is told, as it is my purpose sometime to tell it, men will see what Masonry meant in those awful years, and how nobly it labored against untold odds, in behalf of friendship; even as it labors today, without resting and without lasting, for freedom, gentleness and justice between men and nations.

Nor is Masonry a church, unless we use the word church as Ruskin used it when he said, "There is a true church wherever one hand meets another helpfully, the only holy or mother church that ever was or ever shall be." But if we use the word in its specific sense, Masonry is not a church, nor is it the enemy of any church of any name, seeking instead, to bring men of every faith together the better to teach them to love and honor one another. To that end it invites them to an altar of prayer, laying emphasis only upon that which underlies all creeds and over-arches all sects, while laboring in behalf of that love without which St. Paul said truly that the most perfect theology is nothing. It holds that all true-hearted men are everywhere of one religion, and that when they come to know what they have in common they will discover that they are brethren. Today the religious world, by reason of closer fellowship and a finer courtesy, is moving rapidly toward the Masonic position as set forth in the Constitutions of 1717, and when it arrives Masonry will rejoice in a scene which she has prophesied for ages.

WHAT, THEN, IS MASONRY?

If Masonry is neither a political party nor a religious cult, what, then, is it? It is a world-wide fraternity of God-fearing men, founded upon spiritual faith and moral truth, using the symbols of architecture to teach men the art of building character; a historic fellowship in the search for truth and the service of the ideal, whose sacramental mission is to make men friends and train them in righteousness and liberty. It is, therefore, that it wins the confidence of young men, teaches them to pray to the God whom their fathers trusted, and upon the open Bible which their mothers read asks them to take solemn vows to be good men and true, chaste of heart and charitable of mind, and to build the edifice of their faith and hope and conduct upon the homely old moralities, and to estimate the worth of life by its service and its sanctity. By as much as this spirit prevails, by so much will this sad earth be healed of the wounds of war, the shame of greed and lust and all injustice and unkindness!

> Come, clear the way, then, clear the way;
> Blind creeds and kings have had their day;
> Break the dead branches from the path:
> Our hope is in the aftermath,
> Our hope is in heroic men,
> Star-led to build the world again.
> To this event the ages ran,
> Make way for Brotherhood, make way for Man!

FINIS

ST. LUKE AND EPIPHANY ELECTS DR. NEWTON

New Rector to Take Charge of Church April 1

Election of the Rev. Dr. Joseph Fort Newton as rector of the Episcopal Church of St. Luke and The Epiphany, 13th st. below Spruce, has been announced by the church vestry.

Dr. Newton, a distinguished preacher and author, will assume his new charge on April 1, succeeding the Rev. Thomas L. Harris, who declared his intention to resign about two months ago.

At that time, Mr. Harris expressed dissatisfaction with the progress of the church, and recommended its merger with some other church or a removal to a more favorable location because of the drift of church families away from the center of the city.

Dr. Newton came to this city in 1925 as rector of St. Paul's Church, Overbrook, and in 1930 he became co-rector of St. James' Church, 22d and Walnut sts. He resigned, retaining the status of a special preacher, three years ago, when a merger of St. James and the 13th and Spruce sts. church was being contemplated.

He entered the ministry as a Baptist and later held Congregationalist and Universalist church charges, including the pastorate of City Temple, London, before becoming an Episcopalian.

Mr. Harris told the congregation yesterday that he has "no definite plans" at present. He will introduce Dr. Newton to the congregation on March 13.

COMES TO ST. LUKE'S

REV. JOSEPH FORT NEWTON
Former co-rector of St. James Church will become rector of the Protestant Episcopal Church of St. Luke and the Epiphany on April 1

Dr. Newton had a keen appreciation of good music and as a result our choir was deeply entrenched in his heart. He frequently spoke of it with pride and affection. Also, he thought he had the best vestry of any church in the world. Of course, he did not. He felt this way because we all loved him so, and not once at any meeting of our vestry would anyone question his slightest desire.

Loyal to Dr. Newton's churchmanship, the Church of St. Luke and The Epiphany will continue to be open to all at all times. As befits its namesake, St. Luke the beloved physician, our church will continue to minister to the spiritually sick, regardless of race, creed or color, or of membership or non-membership in any other church—all are cordially welcome to pray and worship with us.

I want to comfort you by saying that Dr. Newton passed away quickly, silently and without pain. He was surrounded by his family, and had sweetly smiled, shortly before his passing, at a compliment made about him by his "baby" Josephine to her mother, "Mother, have you ever seen Daddy look so handsome!" Within the hour he was gone!

I would now like to leave with you one of Dr. Newton's favorite prayers—as indeed, it is of much of mankind—a "Life-Prayer", as he called it, by St. Francis of Assisi:

"Lord make me an instrument of Thy peace; where there is hatred, let me sow love; where there is injury, pardon; where there is doubt, faith; where there is despair, hope; where there is darkness, light; and where there is sadness, joy.

O Divine Master, grant that I may not so much seek to be consoled as to console; to be understood, as to understand; to be loved as to love; for it is in giving that we receive, it is in pardoning that we are pardoned, and it is in dying that we are born to eternal life. Amen."

And now in closing—Of one of Dr. Newton's little masterpieces of literature that has travelled the world over, "Altar Stairs", he says—"A little book that softly talks with God". I would like to use that expression at this time and remind you that I know—and you know—and all the world knows, who knew Dr. Newton—that at this very moment he is cradled in those "everlasting arms"—softly talking with God!

In final tribute to Dr. Newton, may I ask that we join in a moment of silent prayer.

TRIBUTE TO THE REV. JOSEPH FORT NEWTON, D.D.

By

Russell S. Boles, M. D.

*Delivered at the Church of St. Luke and The Epiphany,
Sunday, January 29, 1950.*

It is with inexpressible sorrow that I appear before you this morning, on behalf of the Vestry, to pay tribute to Dr. Newton. I can assure you it is no easy matter to pay appropriate tribute to a man of such stature and attainments! I accept the responsibility with due humility.

I know I should not be full of sorrow—nor should you—that would make Dr. Newton unhappy. So let's talk about him with peaceful hearts. To help us do this I would like to repeat the words of Bishop Armstrong when he walked over to Mrs. Newton, weeping at the side of the grave, and in one of the grandest gestures I have ever seen, said to her, "Joe is going to be all right—what's all the trouble?" And Joe is all right! He had a profound unshakable faith in the immortal life—about this he never wavered, although he often said he doubted his worthiness for it. His favorite text which provided him with so much comfort and which he so many times commended to us, was "The eternal God is thy refuge, and underneath are the everlasting arms." To use his words, "Here is the final security and solace of the little, infinite soul of man in God, only God—God first, God last. He hath made us and not we ourselves. All souls are mine, are his haunting words on the lips of a prophet. Soon or late for all of us the bottom drops out of life. Blinded by some blow, we seem to lose hold of everything—then we discover something that will not let us go; underneath are the everlasting arms, strong, tender, tenacious."

The seed of his immortal faith in the immortal life was planted in the open grave of his father when he was a little lad of six and a half years of age. He could not, and would not believe, at that tender age, that the thud of the dirt upon his father's coffin intoned the end of everything—of all life. The words of the old country minister took hold of him, and he never forgot the power of those words, "I am the resurrection and the life—Let not your hearts be troubled." As Dr. Newton said, "It was as if a great, gentle hand, stronger than the hand of man, and more tender than the hand of any woman, had been put forth from the unseen to caress and heal my spirit." From that day on he never ceased to love Jesus, beyond the power of words to tell.

I do not propose to recount to you the many facts of Dr. Newton's life that established his reputation as a brilliant scholar and author, as a world citizen, as a devout humanitarian, and as one of the greatest preachers in the land. As a preacher, he was, of course, a genius. Hendrik Van Loon has said genius is a perfection of technique, plus something else—some call it God—some call it divine inspiration. In the case of Dr. Newton, there could be no doubt what that "something else" was.

Rather then, than telling you about all the books, magazine articles, sermons and essays he wrote, about his honorary degrees, and all such things, I want to take you for a short time behind the scenes in his life, going back to his early boyhood days—reciting to you, the while, the influences that worked to bring him to the peak of his character and accomplishments—because Dr. Newton was not just an extraordinary man—he was a symbol—a symbol of all that was noble and precious in life. He was a man of ineffable gentleness, and in this gentleness lay an unfathomable influence which molded the lives of those he touched, a quality which made him akin to Lincoln, whom he so vastly admired. His soul was of such a transcendent nature that any attempt to portray it in words would be utterly futile. And what made him this way . . .

He was born in Decatur, Texas. His father was Lee Newton, a Baptist minister, who later became an eminent member of the legal profession. Dr. Newton never knew why his father left the ministry. He lost him at an early age and the poignancy of the loss always lingered. His mother was truly a remarkable woman. She was a college graduate and a musician of merit, teaching music after the loss of her husband in order to keep the little family together. She was a devout Christian and a student of the Bible, the reading of which was a daily ritual in their home. She taught him Latin, Greek, and English literature. He never tired of her reading the plays of Shakespeare and the works of Dickens—so much the latter, that David

Copperfield, Martin Chuzzelwit, Mr. Micawber and the others, were characters as familiar to him as his Texas neighbors. Dr. Newton was tenderly passionate about his little mother. He spoke of her frequently from the pulpit—never without his voice breaking—and, I am sure he worshipped her next to God.

It is said that some men are born great, some achieve greatness and others have greatness thrust upon them. Verily, Dr. Newton was born great. He was born to be a great preacher. Of this there could be no doubt. What a sight to have seen this lad each Sunday on his return home from church with his mother, reenacting the service, standing on a chair as his pulpit, and over the back of it preaching to his little make-believe congregation. The sermon would be complete including all the exhortations and gestures of the village preacher in his most tempestuous moods. His decision to enter the ministry was final when he overheard his mother in one of her daily prayers. Of this experience he said, "She was lifting my life before God, detaining it there, invoking His guidance and blessing upon me."

It was not long before Dr. Newton chafed under the stinging, threatening theological dogmas of his day. As was his nature, he could not perceive a God given to wrath and indignation—only, and always, a loving, forgiving, merciful God. The petty quarrelings in the churches about their creeds and doctrines greatly disturbed him, with the result that then and there he became impatient with sectarianism and determined to apply himself to breaking down its rigid, ugly walls and strive for a universal Church—a goal he never abandoned. Earnestly and energetically he carried on toward this goal beginning as a youth in his first pastorate at Rose Hill, Whiteside County, Texas—then on to the Non-Sectarian Church in St. Louis—the Liberal Christian Church in Cedar Rapids, Iowa—and to the City Temple of London. Impelled by an intense patriotism, he returned to his own country to the Memorial Church of St. Paul in Overbrook—subsequently to St. James Church in Philadelphia and finally to the Church of St. Luke and The Epiphany. Here he spent his last and happiest years—to the end a heroic, liberal churchman.

He was prevailed upon by Bishop Garland to join the Episcopal Church because "something deep in me responds to the sweet and tempered ways of the Episcopal Church. Its atmosphere of reverence, its ordered and stately worship, its tradition of historic continuity, linking today with ages agone; its symbols which enshrine the faith of the past and the hope of the future; its wise and wide tolerance; its old and lovely liturgy—like a stairway, worn by many feet, whereon men climb to God—and still more, the organized mysticism of its sacraments—all these things of beauty and grace move me profoundly."

IN GOD'S KEEPING

The Rev. Joseph Fort Newton, rector of the Church of St. Luke and the Epiphany, 330 S. 13th Street, died suddenly at his home in Merion on January 24th and was buried from the Church on January 27th.

Born in Texas in 1876, son of a Baptist minister, he had earned for himself an enviable reputation as preacher and author before entering the ministry of the Episcopal Church in 1926, when he was ordained by the late Bishop Garland. Since then he confined his ministry to the Diocese of Pennsylvania, serving as rector of St. Paul's Church, Overbrook, co-rector of St. James Church, 22nd and Walnut Streets, and since 1938 rector of the Church of St. Luke and the Epiphany.

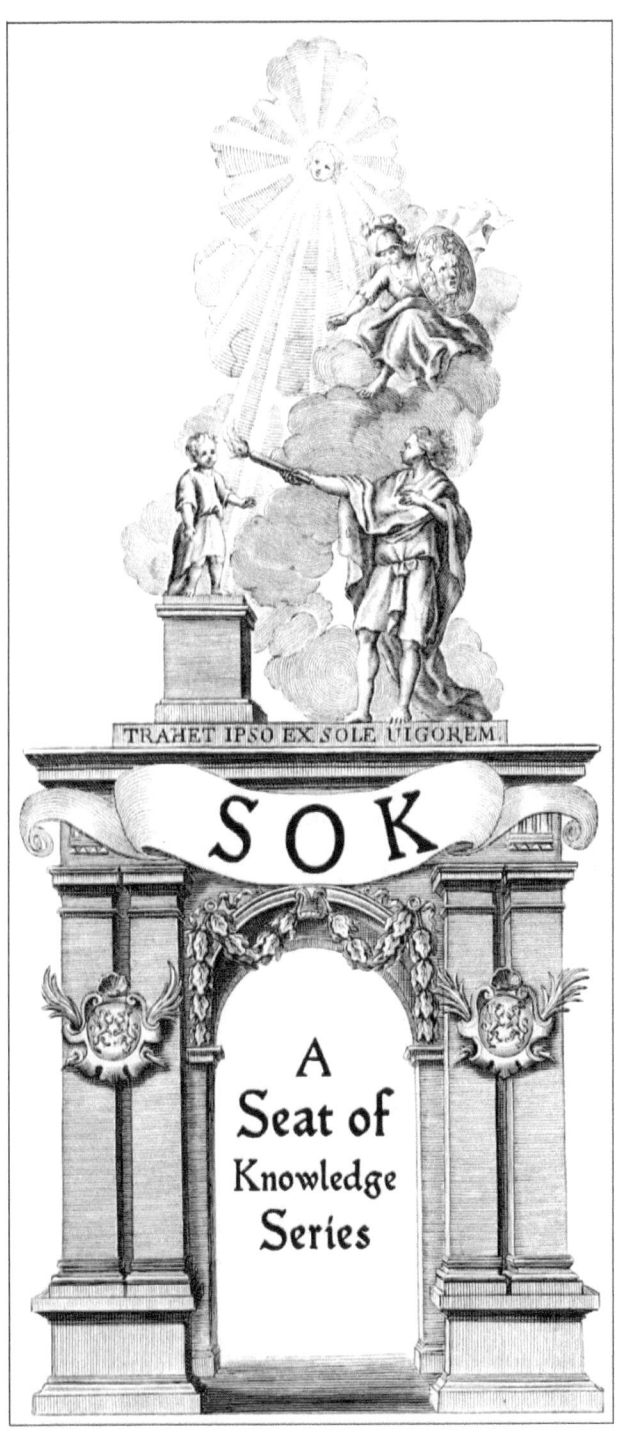

Other Books by the Managing Editor

Manly P. Hall All-Seeing Eye Series:

Book First, Second, Third

Manly P. Hall Seeker of More Intelligent Life Series:

Book I-IV

Hiram E. Buttler Exoteric Christianity

Arthur Waite Forgotten Essays

The Initiates Speak

George Oliver Masonic Writings

Walter L. Wilmshurst Forgotten Essays

Joseph Fort Newton Masonic Writings

H. Stanley Redgrove Forgotten Essays

Freemasons – South Dakota Territory, Book A – K

Freemasons – South Dakota Territory, Book L - Z

For latest books, please visit:

Parallel47North.com/collections/esoteric-books

Contact: Info@Parallel47North.com

About Managing Editor

Darrell Jordan is an acolyte of the August Fraternity, former Noble Grand-IOOF and Freemason.

He is also a member of the Theosophical and Philalethes Societies.

Darrell Jordan